Apostles and Martyrs

Apostles and Martyrs

Peter R S Milward

Gracewing.

First published in 1997

Gracewing
Fowler Wright Books
2 Southern Avenue, Leominster
Herefordshire HR6 0QF

All rights reserved. No part of this publication may be reproduced, stored in a retrieval system, or transmitted in any form, or by any means, electronic, mechanical, photocopying, recording, or otherwise, without the written permission of the publisher.

© Peter R S Milward 1997

The right of Peter R S Milward to be identified as the author of this work has been asserted in accordance with the Copyright, Designs and Patents Act 1988.

ISBN 0 85244 390 0

Typesetting by Action Typesetting Ltd,
Gloucester, GL1 1SP

Printed by Redwood Books
Trowbridge, Wiltshire BA14 8RN

Acknowledgements and Thanks

Some years have passed since I wrote this book, based on translations either from Greek or from Latin. Now that it is to be published I can no longer recollect which source I used for which saint or martyr; and a considerable search through the shelves of the Catholic Central Library in London has only partially solved the problem of identification.

Clearly the earlier parts are based on the New Testament, mainly on the Acts of the Apostles, but I have not aimed at consistency in the versions quoted, and in some cases I may have paraphrased.

The accounts of Ignatius of Antioch and of Polycarp of Smyrna were drawn from Maxwell Staniforth's translation from the Greek, published by Penguin Classics in their 'Early Christian Writings' in 1968 and often reprinted since then. For Justin and Irenaeus I have read, in translation, some of their own writings. My account of the trials and execution of the martyrs in Lyon and Vienne, as well as those of Scillium, have been checked against Musurillo's 'The Acts of the Martyrs' published by the Clarendon Press, Oxford in 1972. This last source gives full versions in Greek or Latin, as well as the English translations, of some twenty-eight distinct trials and executions during the Roman Empire, some of individuals but most of groups of martyrs.

Musurillo also gives the full Latin account of Perpetua and her companions, seemingly written largely by herself (Chapters 3 to 10) and her fellow martyr, Saturus (Chapters 11 to 13), with two introductory chapters and the concluding seven chapters by an eye-witness who may have been Tertullian.

I have read for myself Cyprian's book on the 'Unity of the Church' in a translation by Maurice Bevenot S.J. and of his letters translated by – I believe – Sister Rose Bernard Donna C.S.J. The former of these two is my authority for the explanation of the omission of the word 'primacy' in Cyprian's own revision of Chapter 4 on 'Unity'.

The last section of my book is summarised from Saint Athanasius' 'Life of Saint Antony' translated by Dr R.C. Gregg and published in the 'Oxford Early Christian Texts' series.

To all the translators mentioned above I am deeply indebted and most sincerely grateful.

Contents

Foreword by the Archbishop of Southwark — xi

A Note on Dates — xii

1. **Peter and Paul**
   Pentecost — 1
   Saint Peter (I) *In Jerusalem* — 2
   Saint Stephen — 5
   Saint Peter (II) *The Roman Centurion* — 6
   Saint Peter (III) *Herod Agrippa* — 9
   Saint Peter (IV) *Jewish and Non-Jewish Christians* — 10
   The Council in Jerusalem — 12
   Saint Peter (V) *In Antioch and Rome* — 13
   Saint Paul (I) *The Persecutor* — 14
   Saint Paul (II) *Conversion* — 15
   Saint Paul (III) *In Antioch* — 17
   Saint Paul (IV) *In Asia Minor* (Turkey) — 17
   Saint Paul (V) *The Council in Jerusalem* — 20
   Saint Paul (VI) *In Macedonia* — 21
   Saint Paul (VII) *In Athens and Corinth* — 24
   Saint Paul (VIII) *In Ephesus, Jerusalem and Ephesus again* — 27
   Saint Paul (IX) *Trouble in Corinth and Ankara* — 30
   Saint Paul (X) *To Jerusalem again* — 31
   Saint Paul (XI) *In Jerusalem* — 33
   Saint Paul (XII) *Arrest* — 34
   Saint Paul (XIII) *Conspiracy* — 36

viii Apostles and Martyrs

    Saint Paul (XIV) *Imprisonment in Caesarea, Appeal to Caesar*   38
    Saint Paul (XV) *The Journey to Rome*   40
    Saint Paul (XVI) *Malta and Rome*   42
    Saint Paul (XVII) *Evangelisation from Prison*   43
    Saint Paul (XVIII) *Last Years and Martyrdom*   44
    Saint Paul (XIX) The Apostle, *His Mission and Endurance*   45

A Note on Authors and Authority   48
A Note on Witnesses and Evidence   49

2. Evangelists
    Saint James' Letter   51
    Saints Matthew, Mark and Luke   52
    Saint Peter's Letters   55
    The Letter to the Hebrews   56
    Saint John (I) *Revelation*   56
    Saint John (II) *The Gospel*   58
    Saint John (III) *The Epistles of John*   59

3. Ignatius and Polycarp
    Roman Persecution (I) *Nero, Domitian and Trajan*   63
    Saint Ignatius   64
    Saint Polycarp (I) *Flight and Capture*   66
    Saint Polycarp (II) *Trial and Death*   69

4. Justin and Irenaeus
    Roman Persecution (II) *From Trajan to Marcus Aurelius*   73
    Saint Justin   75
    The Martyrs of Lyon and Vienne   78
    Saint Irenaeus   81
    The Martyrs of Scillium   84

5. Perpetua and her Companions
    Roman Persecution (III) *Septimius Severus*   85
    Saint Perpetua (I) *Arrest*   85
    Saint Perpetua (II) *Prison*   86

Saint Perpetua (III) *Trial*	87
Saint Perpetua (IV) *Dinocrates*	88
Saint Perpetua (V) *Saint Pomponius*	88
Saint Saturus' Vision	89
Saint Felicity	89
Saint Perpetua (VI) *The Games*	90

6. Tertullian and Origen
Tertullian	93
Clement of Alexandria	94
Origen	94

7. Hippolytus
Saint Hippolytus (I) *Quarrel with the Popes*	97
Saint Hippolytus (II) *'The Apostolic Tradition'*	99
Novatian's Schism	100

8. Cyprian and the Popes
Saint Cyprian (I) *The Persecution of Decius*	101
Saint Cyprian (II) *Penance for the Lapsed*	102
Saint Cyprian (III) *The Unity of the Church*	104
Saint Cyprian (IV) *Rome, Africa, Spain, France*	105
Saint Cyprian (V) *Baptism by Heretics*	107
Saint Cyprian (VI) *The Unity of the Bishops*	108
Saint Cyprian (VII) *The Persecution of Valerian*	109
Saint Cyprian (VIII) *Martyrdom*	110

9. Dionysius of Alexandria, Gregory Thaumaturgus, Felix of Nola
Martyrologies	113
Saint Apollonia	114
Saint Dionysius of Alexandria	114
The Martyrs of the Plague	115
Saint Gregory Thaumaturgus	115
Saint Felix of Nola	116

10. The Great Persecution
Years of Peace	119
The Great Persecution (I) *Diocletian*	120
Eusebius (I) *Saint Pamphilus*	122

The Great Persecution (II) *Nine Emperors* 123
Constantine and Christianity 124

11. The Arian Heresy
Saint Lucian and Arius 127
Eusebius (II) *The Council of Nicea* 128
Eusebius (III) *Sabellianism* 129
Saint Athanasius and the Arians 129
Eusebius (IV) *In Praise of Constantine* 130

12. Antony
Saint Antony (I) *Family* 133
Saint Antony (II) *Vocation* 133
The Ascetic Life 134
Saint Antony (III) *Attacks of the Devils* 135
Saint Antony (IV) *In the Cemetery* 136
Saint Antony (V) *In the Fort* 136
Saint Antony (VI) *Recognising Spirits* 137
Saint Antony (VII) *In Alexandria* 138
Saint Peter of Alexandria 139
Saint Antony (VIII) *To the Inner Mountain* 139
Saint Antony (IX) *Teacher and Leader* 140
Saint Antony (X) *In Alexandria again* 141
Saint Antony (XI) *Last Years* 142
Saint Antony (XII) *The Physician of Egypt* 143
Saint Antony (XIII) *Happy Death* 144
The Age of the Fathers of the Church 145

ARCHBISHOP'S HOUSE
ST GEORGE'S ROAD
SOUTHWARK
LONDON SE1 6HX

Foreword

by

His Grace the Archbishop of Southwark

Peter Milward has provided in his book, *Apostles and Martyrs*, a fascinating and highly readable account of key people in the earliest centuries of the Church.

All Christians are familiar with the names of Saints Peter and Paul, and the Evangelists, but far less well known are people who followed later, such as Justin, Irenaeus, Tertullian, Origen and Hippolytus. All these, and others who also played a significant role in the Church in that period, and whose influence is still with us today, are included here.

This book is informative without being 'heavy', and provides a splendid introduction to the life and times of people to whom we owe a debt of gratitude for their heroic witness to Christ and to the truth of the Christian Faith.

✝ Michael Bowen

Archbishop of Southwark

A Note on Dates

As this book is about real people and real things it gives the real places and dates of what happened as far as possible. We know about these people and what they did because some of them wrote what they themselves had seen and listened to during their own lifetime. Others wrote soon after the death of the people concerned.

The Christian writers in the time of the apostles and during the next two hundred years did not usually note down exact dates, so later people have had to study all the circumstances to work them out. The dates in this book have been worked out carefully; they are probably correct or nearly correct. The year of Christ's death and resurrection may have been AD 33, but AD 30 seems more likely.

Up to about 1500 years ago writers used different ways of counting years. In Rome they counted from the year when they thought the city was first built. In year 1278 from the founding of Rome, Pope John the First asked a monk called Dionysius the Small to check on methods of fixing the date of Easter each year. While Dionysius was working on this he thought it would be better to count all the years from the birth of our Lord, because that was a more important event than the founding of Rome.

Saint Luke had written that John the Baptist began his preaching and baptising 'in the fifteenth year of the reign of the Emperor Tiberius'. This was the year 783 from the founding of Rome. Luke also wrote that Jesus, when he was baptised by John and began his public work, was 'about thirty years old'. So Dionysius subtracted 30 from 783 and took Roman year 753 as the year when our Lord was born. He did not check on the dates of Herod the Great. It was Herod the Great who had had all the babies in Bethlehem killed to try to make sure that our Lord would not become king. This Herod died in Roman year 749 (or 750) so Dionysius was about four or five years wrong. Saint Luke wrote that our Lord was at that time *about* thirty'. We reckon he may have been thirty-four or thirty-five.

Other Christian writers after Dionysius found his 'In the Year of the Lord ... ' dates (in Latin, 'Anno Domini' or 'AD') so convenient that they began to use them too – but still without checking the Roman records to see when Herod the Great had died.

Saint Bede, who lived from 672 to 735 (more than a hundred years after Dionysius the Small) wrote a History of the Church in England. As a historian he found Dionysius' way of dating most useful. He may have realised that our Lord was actually born four or five years earlier than Dionysius had reckoned, but the new dates were already widely used so he did not make any change. Bede's History and his other books were very popular. Soon in all the countries of Europe, and nowadays throughout the world, the AD dates are used for everything that has happened since the time of our Lord.

1

Peter and Paul

Pentecost

On Friday, 7th April, in the year AD 30 our Lord died on the cross just outside Jerusalem. On Sunday, the 9th, he rose again. During forty days he showed himself to his apostles, and to his friends and followers, in Jerusalem, on the roads, by the lake of Galilee and in other places. He spoke to them as friends and as a family, sometimes eating with them; and he gave them last instructions about the Church he had founded in them. He told Peter that he was to be the shepherd and leader of the Church, and that when he was old he would be killed. He told them he was going back to God the Father. They were to wait in Jerusalem for him to send them the Holy Spirit. He told them that after that they should go out to teach all nations and to baptise people in the name of the Father and of the Son and of the Holy Spirit. Then on Thursday, 18th May, he went up to heaven in front of their eyes, promising to come again in clouds of glory at the Last Judgement. Our Lady, the apostles and their closest friends stayed in Jerusalem praying during the next ten days.

On Sunday, 28th May, the Holy Spirit came down on them like flames of fire, with the noise of a great wind. That day is sometimes called the birthday of the Church. So far as we know, the only people before that Sunday whom we would call Christians were the five hundred or so to whom our Lord had shown himself after his resurrection. But, with the strength of the Holy Spirit, Peter and the apostles began to speak to the crowds. Many of the people had seen Jesus before he was killed and had heard him speak. Others already knew something about him. By the end of that first day, with the power of the Holy Spirit, a great number were ready to believe fully in our Lord and to follow him. The Church had begun to grow and the apostles had baptised about three thousand people in one day.

At that first Pentecost in AD 30 the Christians, although they were all Jews, did not all speak the same language. Those who lived in Judea would usually speak Aramaic. If they came from Galilee they would also be able to speak and understand Greek, although most of them would have difficulty in writing it. But at Pentecost many Jews came to Jerusalem from places further away, where they did not speak either of these languages properly; yet that day, by the power of the Holy Spirit, the apostles were able to speak so that they could all understand in their own language and dialect.

In the days and weeks that followed, the new Christians all kept together, sharing their food and money, but those who could only speak Greek sometimes felt left out; so the apostles chose seven speakers of good Greek to look after them. They prayed for them and laid their hands on them, ordaining them for a special ministry as helpers for the apostles. We call them the first 'deacons'.

When they spoke to the crowds in Jerusalem they told them that Jesus, whom the chief priests and the leaders of the Jews had had killed, was the saviour and the Son of God. Those Jews who believed were truly sorry and joined the Christians. But those who refused to believe were angry because the apostles said that their chief priests were murderers who had killed the Son of God. Some of the priests themselves became Christians. This made the others more angry and they started a persecution.

Saint Peter (I)
In Jerusalem

The apostles and the other Christians still went to the temple every day to pray; but they celebrated the Eucharist (the 'Breaking of Bread' they called it then) in their own houses.

As our Lord had promised, there were many miracles and signs worked through them. One day, when Peter and John were going to the Temple at the time of the evening sacrifice, a man was carried past them, a cripple who could not walk. He was carried every day to the gate called the 'Beautiful Gate' so that he could beg from the people going in. When he saw Peter and John going in to the Temple he begged them for money. Peter and John said, 'Look at us'. Peter went on, 'I have no money, silver nor gold, but what I have I will give you. In the name of Jesus of Nazareth, walk.' At once the man's legs were cured. He jumped up, stood and went into the Temple with them, walking and jumping and praising God.

Many people recognised the man; they were astonished to see him walking. Everyone came running up in great excitement and crowded round in the Portico of Solomon where the man was still clinging to Peter and John; so Peter said to them, 'Why are you staring at us as though we had made this man walk by our own power? It is because we believe in Jesus that God has restored this man to health. You and your leaders handed Jesus over to Pilate. You accused him who was holy and just. You asked for a murderer to be released instead. All the prophets from Moses and Samuel said these things would happen. You are the heirs of the prophets and of God's covenant with Abraham. It was for you first of all that God raised up his servant and sent him to you so that you should turn away from wickedness.'

While they were talking the priests came up to them with the captain of the Temple guard and the Sadducees. The Sadducees did not believe that the dead will rise again; so they were especially angry with the apostles for saying that Christ had risen and that we too shall rise at the last day. They arrested Peter and John, and put them in prison for the night.

Next day the high priests and their families called them in for questioning. Peter answered, 'You are asking us about an act of kindness to a cripple, and how he was cured. I am glad to tell you and would be glad to tell all the people of Israel. He was cured by the name of Jesus of Nazareth, the one whom you killed and whom God raised from the dead.'

The priests were astonished at the courage of Peter and John. They sent the two of them outside while they had a private discussion. Some of the priests said, 'It is obvious to everyone in Jerusalem that a miracle has been worked by these people in public. We cannot deny it.' They could not think of any excuse to punish them, so they agreed to tell them not to speak about Jesus in public; then they released them.

The apostles went on telling people about Jesus Christ and how he had risen from the dead. When they heard about the cripple and other miracles more people began to come, to see and listen. They even brought sick men and women out onto the streets on beds and sleeping mats so that Peter's shadow could touch them as he went past. Others came from outside Jerusalem to be cured. At last the high priest and his supporters stepped in again. They arrested the apostles and put them in prison once more.

This time an angel of God opened the prison gates during the night and let them out. Then, when the officials were sent next morning to bring the apostles to court, the men came back saying, 'We found the prison locked with the warders on duty, but when we unlocked the door there was no one inside'. Then someone came in from the Temple and said, 'At this very moment those men you imprisoned are back in the Temple teaching the people'.

The captain and his men went again to the Temple. They dared not arrest the apostles there because the people might have rioted and stoned them. But the apostles voluntarily went back with them to the high priest. The high priest said to them, 'We warned you not to teach in this name, and what have you done? You have filled all Jerusalem with your teaching. You seem determined to make out that we murdered him.' Peter answered, 'We must obey God before we obey men. It was God who raised up Jesus. It was you who had him executed, nailed to a tree. God has raised him up to be a leader and saviour, to make us Jews repent and to bring us forgiveness. We are witnesses to all this – we and the Holy Spirit, which God has given to us who follow him.'

The priests were furious. They wanted to kill them. But one Pharisee called Gamaliel, who was a master and teacher of the Law, respected by everyone, asked for the apostles to be taken outside again. He then gave the priests examples of other teachers and leaders who had had many followers; but their movements had all petered out. 'I suggest', he said, 'you leave these men alone and let them go. If this movement is just another, led by men, it will break up by itself. But if it comes from God you will not be able to stop it. You might find yourselves fighting against God.'

They followed his advice. They called the apostles in, had them flogged, told them again not to teach people about Jesus, and let them go. The apostles were glad to have had the honour of suffering something for Jesus' sake.

Saint Stephen

All this time they went on preaching. The number of Christians grew from three thousand to five thousand, from five thousand to many more. A large group of Temple priests joined them. The seven deacons, who had been ordained to help the apostles, also began to teach. Among the seven God gave special grace and power to Stephen. He worked miracles and signs; he preached to the Greek-speaking Jews in Greek. But some of these Jews from one of the Greek-speaking synagogues in Jerusalem started a public argument with him. They found they could not get the better of him. He was very wise and God helped him; so they got some men to tell lies against him, to say that Stephen spoke against Moses, or against the Temple, or against the Law. They took him by surprise, arrested him and led him to the court of the high priests.

The high priest asked Stephen if it was true that he said such things. Stephen told them, starting from Abraham, how the Jews again and again had persecuted God's prophets, and how at last they had killed the Son of God. 'Now you have become his betrayers, his murderers. You who had God's Law brought to you by angels are the very ones who have broken the Law.'

They were so angry at this that they dragged Stephen out of the city and stoned him to death. As he was dying he prayed,

'Lord Jesus, receive my spirit. Lord, do not hold this sin against them.'

That day began a bitter persecution against the Christians. It was so bad that many of them, especially those who spoke Greek, left Jerusalem to stay in the country parts of Judea and in Samaria.

Saint Peter (II)
The Roman Centurion

Philip, another of the first seven deacons, began preaching and baptising in Samaria. When the apostles in Jerusalem heard this they sent Peter and John to Samaria to confirm the Samaritans whom Philip had baptised. They laid their hands on them and the Samaritan Christians too received the Holy Spirit.

Around this time, perhaps eight or ten years after our Lord's resurrection and ascension, the persecution died down. The apostles and other Christians went through the towns and villages of Judea, Samaria and Galilee, spreading the good news of Christ among all kinds of Jews, baptising them and confirming them with the Holy Spirit.

Saint Peter especially travelled round Israel, preaching and often working miracles. At Lydda, about twenty-five miles from Jerusalem, he cured a man called Aeneas who had been paralysed and bedridden for eight years. Everybody who lived in Lydda saw him and they were all converted.

In Jaffa, the seaport twelve miles from Lydda (it is now a suburb of Tel Aviv), a very good, kind woman called Tabitha in Aramaic (Dorcas in Greek) had died. Her body was washed and laid out for burial. When her friends heard that Peter was in Lydda they sent two men to ask him to visit Jaffa as soon as possible. Peter went back with them at once. When he arrived they took him up to the room where all her friends were standing round Dorcas' body and crying. They showed him the jackets and clothes which Dorcas had been making, but Peter sent them out of the room. He knelt down and prayed. Then he turned to Dorcas and said, 'Tabitha, stand up.' She opened her eyes, looked at Peter and sat up.

Peter helped her to her feet and called the others back in. The whole town heard about it and many believed in our Lord.

One day while Peter was in Jaffa, in the house of Simon the tanner, he went up at mid-day onto the flat roof to pray. He was hungry, looking forward to his lunch, when God showed him a vision. He saw the sky open and a great sheet was let down by its four corners. In it were all kinds of animals and birds. He heard a voice saying, 'Now Peter, kill something and eat'.

According to Jewish rules Jews are not allowed to eat any meat unless it is 'kosher'. Kosher meat is killed in a special way by a special butcher and served on special dishes so that it will not be 'unclean'. So Peter said, 'Certainly not, Lord. I have never eaten anything unclean.'

The voice said, 'What God has made clean you must not call unclean'. This was repeated three times; then the sheet was taken up again to the sky.

The day before Peter's vision, in the afternoon, a Roman centurion called Cornelius, a captain in the Roman army, stationed at Caesarea thirty miles away from Jaffa, had also had a vision. He was not a Jew, though he, with all his family and servants, believed in God. He constantly prayed. That day he saw an angel of God come to the house and call him. He was terrified. He stared at the angel and said, 'What is it, Lord?'

The angel said, 'Your prayers and the money you give to him and to the poor have been accepted by God. Now you must send someone to Jaffa and fetch a man called Simon Peter. He is staying with Simon the tanner. His house is by the sea.'

When the angel had gone Cornelius called two of his servants and a capable, religious soldier. He told them what had happened and sent them to Jaffa. It was just as they were coming into Jaffa next day that Peter had his vision. He was still worrying over the meaning of the vision by the time they had asked their way and reached the door of the house. The Holy Spirit had to tell Peter, 'Some men have come to see you. Hurry down; and don't hesitate about going back with them. It was I who told them to come.' So Peter went down and said to them, 'I am the man you are looking for. Why did you come?'

They told Peter what a good man Cornelius was and how the Jews respected him. 'He was directed', they said, 'by a holy angel to send for you, to bring you to his house and to listen to what you had to say'. So Peter asked them in and had them stay with him that night. Next day he set off with them and with some of the Christians of Jaffa. The day after that they reached Caesarea where Cornelius was waiting for them. He had asked his relations and close friends to be there too.

As Peter and the others reached the house Cornelius went out and knelt, bowing his head to the ground in front of Peter. But Peter caught hold of him. 'Stand up', he said, 'I'm only a man'. So Cornelius took him to meet all the people who had come to hear him

'You know', said Peter, 'we Jews are forbidden to mix with people who are not Jews. But God has shown me that I must not call anyone unclean. Before I explain I should like to know why you sent for me.' Cornelius then told him of the vision of the shining angel and how glad he was that Peter had agreed to come. 'We are all here', he said, 'to hear from you what message God has given you for us'.

'I realise now', replied Peter, 'that God doesn't have favourites. Anybody of any nationality who fears God and does right is welcomed by God. It is true that God sent his word to the people of Israel first. It was to them, the Jews, that Jesus Christ brought the good news of peace. You must have heard of what has been happening in Jerusalem, and about John who preached and baptised people, and Jesus of Nazareth after John – how he started in Galilee and went about doing good. Now I, and these people with me, saw everything and can tell you everything he did in Judea and in Jerusalem, and how they killed him, crucifying him on a tree. Yet three days afterwards God raised him to life. He allowed his chosen witnesses to see him. We are those witnesses. We ate and drank with him after he rose from the dead. He has told us to tell this to all his people; to tell them that God has made him judge of everyone, living and dead. All the prophets told us about this beforehand. All who believe in Jesus will have their sins forgiven through him.'

Suddenly, while Peter was speaking, the Holy Spirit came

down on Cornelius and the other Romans, just as he had on the apostles, the first Jewish Christians, in Jerusalem. After that, as Peter said, they could not hesitate. He had them all baptised, and in this way the first pagans – the first non-Jews – joined the Church.

Peter stayed with them some days. When he went back to Jerusalem some of the Jewish Christians blamed him for visiting pagans and eating with them. So Peter explained to them what had happened in Jaffa and Caesarea. At length they were satisfied and gave glory to God. 'This shows', they said, 'that God can give even the pagans the grace of repentance and eternal life'.

This was important because some of those Christians who had left Jerusalem at the time of the persecution on account of Stephen had gone to Antioch in Syria. There a number of the pagan Greeks had begun to believe in Jesus Christ and had joined the Christians. The Church in Jerusalem sent Barnabas to Antioch to see how God was with them there and to confirm them as Christians.

Saint Peter (III)
Herod Agrippa

Herod the Great, who heard from the wise men about our Lord's birth, had died in 4 BC. One of his sons was Herod – Herod Antipas – who had had John the Baptist killed. It was to Herod Antipas that Pilate sent our Lord in AD 30, trying to get out of the responsibility for our Lord's trial. Still another Herod, a grandson of Herod the Great, was made king of Judea and Samaria under the Romans in AD 41. This Herod, Herod Agrippa the First, had the apostle James, the brother of John, beheaded because he thought it would please the Jews. Next he put Peter in prison. He planned to have a public trial after Passover week because he thought this would make him more popular. He ordered four squads of soldiers to guard Peter. All the Christian church in Jerusalem prayed for him continuously.

On the night before the trial was due, Peter was sleeping between two soldiers, handcuffed to them on each side.

Other guards were on duty at the main gate of the prison when suddenly an angel stood near Peter and the prison cell was filled with light. He tapped Peter on the side and woke him. 'Get up,' he said. 'Hurry!' The chains fell off Peter's wrists. 'Put on your belt and sandals,' the angel said. 'Wrap your cloak round you and follow me.' Peter could not believe this was really happening. He thought he was dreaming. They passed through two guard posts, one after the other, and reached the iron gate leading to the city. This opened of its own accord. They went out and walked the length of one street when the angel left him. It was only then that Peter came to himself. 'Now I know it is all true,' he said. 'The Lord really did sent an angel to save me from Herod and from all the things which the Jewish people thought were certain to happen to me.'

When he realised this he went straight to the house of Mary, the mother of John Mark. A number of Christians were meeting there and praying. He knocked on the outside door and a servant called Rhoda came to answer it. She recognised Peter's voice, and she was so excited and happy that she ran back inside, forgetting to let him in. When she told them that Peter was at the door they said, 'You are out of your mind.' She insisted it was true. Then they said, 'It must be his angel.' Peter went on knocking till at last they opened the door and were amazed to see it really was Peter himself. He told them to tell James, our Lord's cousin. It is not clear whether this is the same James as the son of Alpheus who was one of the twelve first apostles. Peter then went away so that the soldiers would not find him – possibly as far as Rome. James stayed in Jerusalem.

These things happened in AD 41 when Herod Agrippa became king, or soon afterwards. This Herod died in AD 44.

Saint Peter (IV)
Jewish and Non-Jewish Christians

During the AD 40s the Church was spreading and new Christians were being baptised, not only in Judea and Samaria but also in Syria, north beyond Galilee. Those Christians who had stayed in Jerusalem after the persecution at the time of Stephen's martyrdom were probably all converted Jews. They continued to keep the rules of the Jewish Law. They took part in the Temple services as well as celebrating the Eucharist in their homes. While Peter and the other apostles travelled around, Saint James, the cousin of our Lord, was head of the church in the city.

(Through parts of Europe, most of the Americas and elsewhere the Eucharistic celebration is now called 'Mass' or 'Missa' from the words of dismissal at the end of the Latin Mass: *Ite, missa est*. In the early Church the celebration was often called the 'Mysteries' because the Christians who had not yet been baptised had to leave after the Readings and any homily. Only after baptism were they admitted to the Consecration and Communion.)

During his travels Peter spent some time in Antioch. At first he used to join the non-Jewish Christians there and eat with them, although this was against the rules of the Jewish Law. But some friends of James came from Jerusalem and persuaded him to stop doing this. They wanted all the new Christians to become like Jews and to be circumcised like Jews before they would all eat together. They said, 'Unless you have yourselves circumcised in the tradition of Moses you cannot be saved'. Other Jewish Christians in Antioch then followed Peter's example. Saint Paul, who was converting many of the pagans and baptising them, said to Peter in front of everyone, 'In spite of being a Jew you live like the pagans and not like the Jews. You have no right to force the pagans to copy Jewish ways.'

This trouble between Jewish and non-Jewish Christians is described by Saint Luke in the Acts of the Apostles, and by Saint Paul in his letter to the Galatians. Paul writes of a visit he made to Jerusalem with Barnabas 'fourteen years' after his conversion. During this visit he told the leading Christians about the 'good news' as he was proclaiming it to the pagans. He did this to check that his teaching was in line with that of the other apostles. He had brought with him to Jerusalem a non-Jewish convert called Titus, and none of the leading Christians in Jerusalem had obliged Titus to be circumcised. They had recognised that Paul had been chosen by our Lord especially to spread the gospel among the pagans while Peter's work was mainly among the Jews. The only thing they had insisted on was that he should remember to help the poor – which he wished to do.

The Council in Jerusalem

Luke, in the Acts of the Apostles at the end of Chapter 11, writes that at the time of the famine in Jerusalem, about AD 49, the Christians in Antioch collected money to help those in Jerusalem, and got Barnabas and Paul to take it there. At the end of Chapter 12 he adds that when they had done this Barnabas and Paul went back to Antioch taking John Mark with them. This visit may be the same as the one which Paul wrote about to the Galatians.

Luke next describes Paul's first missionary journey with Barnabas. This included preaching in two towns in Lycaonia which had been reckoned part of Galatia some time earlier. He then describes (in Chapter 15) the trouble in Antioch between the Jewish and non-Jewish Christians about whether those who had been pagans needed to be circumcised. It was arranged that Paul and Barnabas should go to Jerusalem to discuss the problem with the Christians there. They were welcomed by the apostles and the leaders of the church; but as in Antioch some of the Pharisees who had become Christians argued that the converts should all be circumcised and told to keep the Law of Moses.

There was a long discussion. Peter told them all again how the Holy Spirit had been given to Cornelius and the other pagans. 'It would only make God angry now', he said, 'if you put on the new Christians that burden [of the Law] which neither we nor our ancestors have been strong enough to support'. Then Barnabas and Paul told them of all the signs and wonders which God had worked through them among the pagans. In the end James, whose 'friends' had caused the start of the whole argument, decided that they should send a letter to 'the brothers of pagan birth' in Antioch, giving them a few simple rules about food which would make it easier for the Jewish Christians to eat with them, and telling them not to be anxious about the rest. Two other Jewish Christians, Jude and Silas, went back with Paul and Barnabas, taking this letter to Antioch where all the Christians read it with joy.

Luke's report of this Council of Jerusalem shows it was very important. Paul seems to have made a special journey to Jerusalem for it soon after his visit with the famine relief funds, but it is not mentioned in any of Saint Paul's letters which have survived. His Letter to the Galatians was partly on the same subject. We are not sure of the reason for this. It may be that Paul's letter to Galatia was written before the Council. If so, then either the 'Galatians' he was writing to were the Lycaonians whom he had visited during his first missionary journey (Lycaonia had at one time been reckoned a part of Galatia) or they were converts further north, in Galatia proper, who had learned their Christianity from those already taught by Paul. He went through central Galatia on his next missionary journey from AD 50 to 52.

Saint Peter (V)
In Antioch and Rome

During the years when Paul was travelling we think that Peter settled in Antioch for a time, leaving James as head of the church in Jerusalem. Around the year AD 50 there grew up a Christian church in Rome, the capital of the empire. We do not know who were its first missionaries, but because it was the capital it became the most important centre for the whole of the Church. Eventually Peter transferred his headquarters to Rome. Paul too arrived there as a prisoner under guard in AD 61. While Peter was in Rome Mark joined him and learned from him much of the story of our Lord's public life which Peter had shared. He wrote these up in the little book we now call the Gospel according to Mark.

In AD 64 there was a great fire in Rome; the Emperor Nero tried to make out that the Christians had started it and he began to have them all cruelly killed. It was about this time or soon afterwards that Saint Peter was martyred. Linus and Cletus (or Anacletus) were the next two heads of the church in Rome, followed by Clement. There is a tradition that Peter asked to be crucified upside-down because it would be too great an honour to die upright as our Lord had done. Saint Clement's letter to the Corinthians confirms that Peter died an exemplary death.

Saint Paul (I)
The Persecutor

God has taught us about himself in different ways at different times. His main teaching was through his Son, our Lord, while he was on earth from about 5 BC to AD 30. But God had prepared beforehand for our Lord's coming by teaching the Jews, the descendants of Abraham, through hundreds of years. Our Lord was a Jew, and so were the twelve apostles and the first Christians. But the land where they lived was then part of the pagan Roman Empire. Greek and Latin were the common languages.

The Romans and Greeks believed in many gods, some of whom were more like devils. They tried to make everyone believe in the same gods so as to make it easier to rule the Empire. Julius Caesar, who died in 44 BC, and Caesar Augustus, who died in AD 14, were called gods after they were dead. People were expected to worship them. The Emperors Caligula (died AD 41) and Domitian (died AD 96) expected people to worship them while they were still alive. They punished anyone who refused.

The Christians were persecuted first by Jews and later by the Romans. Most Jews would not recognise that our Lord was the Christ. They had had him killed and sometimes they killed his followers. The Christians would not worship the Greek and Roman gods, so at times the Romans too tortured and killed them. But the Romans respected the Jews for their strict morals and religion. Also, some important Jewish families were useful to the Romans. These families were given special privileges as Roman citizens; and the Jewish religion was one of the few different religions which the Romans allowed people to practice.

Saul of Tarsus came from the town of Tarsus in the corner of the north-eastern Mediterranean (now southern Turkey), from a respected Jewish family. He was a Roman citizen, well educated in Greek. He also studied Jewish Law and history under the famous teacher, Gamaliel. He was a chief persecutor of the Christians at the time of Stephen. He looked after the cloaks of the men who stoned Stephen to death. He went from house to house in Jerusalem, arresting men and women and sending them to prison. Most of the Christians seem to have left the city for a time and some of them made converts, starting fresh churches in the places where they went. Other local churches were started by Jews who had come to Jerusalem from far away for the Jewish feasts, and had been converted before they went home. One important group was in Damascus in Syria. About AD 36 Saul got official letters from the chief priests in Jerusalem, authorising him to arrest all the Christians in Damascus, to send them as prisoners back to Jerusalem to be tried in the court of the Jewish priests. The journey from Jerusalem to Damascus was well over a hundred miles.

Saint Paul (II)
Conversion

Suddenly, while Saul was travelling to Damascus, just before he reached the city, there came a great light from heaven all round him, and he saw our Lord there. He fell to the ground and heard Jesus say, 'Saul, Saul, why are you persecuting me? Get up now. Go into the city. You will be told what you have to do.'

The men travelling with Saul stood speechless. They heard the voice but they could see no one. Saul got up. The light and the vision had blinded him; so they had to lead him by the hand into Damascus. He was blind for three days. During that time he fasted, taking neither food nor drink.

A Christian called Ananias, who lived in Damascus, had a vision of our Lord saying to him, 'Ananias, you must go to the street called Straight Street and ask at the house of Judas for a man called Saul. He comes from Tarsus. At this moment he is praying and seeing a vision of you coming in to lay your hands on him to give him back his sight.'

'Lord,' replied Ananias, 'people have been telling me about this man and all the harm he has been doing to your followers in Jerusalem. He has only come here because he holds a warrant from the chief priests to arrest everyone who believes in you.'

'You must go all the same.' said our Lord. 'This man has been chosen by me to bring my name to pagans, to kings, as well as to the Jews of Israel. I will show him how much he will suffer for my sake.'

Then Ananias went to the house of Judas and laid his hands on Saul's head. 'Brother Saul,' he said, 'I have been sent to you by the Lord Jesus, who appeared to you on your way here, so that you may get back your sight and be filled with the Holy Spirit.'

It seemed as though scales fell from Saul's eyes and he could see again. He was baptised then and there. After taking some food he began to regain his strength. He spent only a few days with the other Christians in Damascus before he began preaching in the synagogue. He now said openly, 'Jesus is the Son of God.' After this he spent some time in Arabia, probably in what is now the kingdom of Jordan.

He seems to have realised right away that God had chosen him specially to bring our Lord to the pagans, so he did not go back at once to Jerusalem but went again to Damascus to teach and preach for one or two years. His power increased steadily. He showed the Jews in Damascus how Jesus was the Christ, the Messiah, whom the prophets had taught them to expect. Many Jews believed, but others became so angry that they worked out a plot to kill him. They set men to watch for him at the city gates, day and night. Saul heard of this so he decided to escape. He was a small man. When it was dark his friends let him down from the top of the city wall in a basket. Then he went to Jerusalem to see Saint Peter.

When he reached Jerusalem he tried to join the disciples but they were all afraid of him. They could not believe that he had really changed so much. Barnabas, however, knew what had happened to him. Barnabas was a Levite who had been born in Cyprus. In the early days of the Church in Jerusalem he had sold a large piece of land which he owned and had brought all the money to the apostles. He was well known to them and they trusted him. He looked after Saul and introduced him to Peter. Saul stayed two weeks with

Peter and met James, our Lord's cousin.

During this short stay in Jerusalem Saul spoke about our Lord to Greek-speaking Jews and an argument began, as it had in Damascus. Again they decided to kill him. Because of this the Christians took him away to Caesarea. There they saw him aboard a ship sailing to Tarsus where he had been born.

Saint Paul (III)
In Antioch

It was a little after this, about AD 43 or 44, that the number of Christians in Antioch was growing so fast that the church in Jerusalem sent Barnabas to see how God was working among them. Barnabas confirmed them and helped them; then he went on to Tarsus to find Saul again. When he found him he brought him back to Antioch. They lived together there for more than a year, teaching, preaching and baptising many more Christians. It was in Antioch that people first used the word 'Christian' to distinguish those who believed in Christ and were baptised.

Other important Christians came from Jerusalem to Antioch. One of them called Agabus was inspired by the Holy Spirit to prophesy. He foretold the famine which occurred about AD 49. It was on account of that famine that Barnabas and Saul took the money collected in Antioch to Jerusalem to help the church there.

Meanwhile, about AD 45 or 46, when they were praying together one day the Holy Spirit showed them that Barnabas and Saul were to take up a special work for God, spreading the Church more widely through the world. The Christians in Antioch prayed for them and fasted. Then they laid their hands on them and sent them off.

Saint Paul (IV)
In Asia Minor (Turkey)

Saul and Barnabas set out by sea with John Mark who was a cousin of Barnabas. They landed first at a place called

Salamis on the island of Cyprus where Barnabas had been born. They travelled the length of Cyprus from east to west, about a hundred miles, teaching in the Jewish synagogues at each place where they stopped. At Paphos the Roman pro-consul, Sergius Paulus, the governor of the island, heard about them and called them in to speak to him. Among the governor's officials was a man called Elymas who claimed to be a magician. He tried to stop the governor from listening; but Saul, or Paul as he is now called, said to him, 'You are a fraud, an imposter. You work for the devil and against true religion. God will blind you for a time so that you will not see the sun.' That instant Elymas found his sight darkened. He groped around for someone to lead him by the hand. The pro-consul, who had been astonished by what he had learned about our Lord, became a Christian.

Next, Paul and his friends went by sea to Perga on the mainland, a hundred and seventy miles or so north-west from Paphos; but John Mark left them there to go back to Jerusalem. At the time Paul called this desertion, though years later Mark and Paul worked together in Rome.

From Perga, Paul and Barnabas went north about ninety miles to another town called Antioch – Antioch in Pisidia, not Antioch in Syria.

On a Saturday, the Jewish Sabbath, they were invited to speak to the Jews in the synagogue. Paul stood up and told them about our Lord. He began the way Stephen had done in Jerusalem ten years earlier. He went through the history of Israel and the prophecies which had prepared them for the coming of Christ. He told them of John the Baptist. It seems that the Jews everywhere had heard about him. He showed them how all their history, their prophets, and John the Baptist's evidence also, all led up to Jesus Christ. 'What the people of Jerusalem and their rulers did, though they did not realise it,' he said, 'was in fact to fulfil the prophecies which are read to us, Sabbath by Sabbath. Though they found no crime in him they condemned him and got Pilate to have him executed. When they had carried out everything the prophets had foretold about him they took him down from the tree and buried him in a tomb. But God raised him from the dead; and for many days he appeared to those who had been with him before. It is these same companions of his who are now his witnesses before our people. We have come here to tell you the good news.

'It was to our ancestors that God made the promise, but it is to us, their children, that he has fulfilled the promise by raising Jesus from the dead. My brothers, I wish you to realise that it is through him that we can have the salvation from our sins which even Moses and the Law could not bring.'

The Jews who listened were deeply interested. Some of them joined Paul and Barnabas at once. Others asked them to preach again the next Saturday. When that Saturday came round almost the whole town came to hear them. This made some of the leading Jews jealous. They contradicted everything Paul and Barnabas said. When the argument became too fierce Paul spoke out. 'We had to tell you first the word of God; but since you reject it – since you do not seem to think you are worthy of eternal life – we will turn to the pagans.'

It made the pagans very happy to hear this. They thanked God for sending them his message. Many became Christians. The news of God's word spread through the countryside. But the jealous Jews worked on some pious rich women and the leading men of the city. They managed to have Paul and Barnabas turned out of the place. The two were happy to feel they were suffering as our Lord had, and they went off east to Iconium, now called Konya, seventy miles away, near the border of Lycaonia.

In Iconium Paul and Barnabas again made many converts; they were able to stay there some time. God supported with his grace all that they said. He allowed them to perform signs and miracles; but again some of the Jews refused to believe. They persuaded pagans also to work against them. They tried to get the police to stay away from the meetings, so that they could organise an attack on them and stone them. When the apostles learned of this they went on to Lystra in Lycaonia, about twenty miles or so to the south.

In Lystra a cripple who had never walked in his life was among those listening to Paul's preaching. He caught his attention. Paul told him, 'Get up, stand up'. The cripple jumped up and began to walk. All the pagans who knew the man had been a cripple were astonished. They said, 'These

are gods who have come to us disguised as men.' As
Barnabas was the taller they called him Zeus, the chief of
the gods. As Paul was the principal speaker they called him
Hermes, the messenger god. The priests of the temple of
Zeus put garlands of leaves on some oxen and brought them
to the city to sacrifice them to Barnabas and Paul. When the
apostles heard what was happening they were horrified. They
rushed into the crowd shouting, 'Friends, what do you think
you are doing? We are only men like you. We have come
with good news. Leave these empty idols of your gods. Turn
to the living God who made heaven and earth and sea and
everything in them. It is he who gives you good things: rain
from heaven, good crops, good food and happiness.' Even
speaking like this was scarcely enough to stop the crowd from
offering their sacrifice.

After some time, once again a number of Jews came from
Antioch in Pisidia and from Iconium, to turn people against
the apostles. This time they caught Paul. They stoned him
and dragged him out of the town, thinking he was dead. The
Christians came crowding round him, but as they did so he
came to himself and stood up. He went back into the town.
Next day he and Barnabas went on to Derbe, about another
thirty miles.

In Derbe they preached again and made more new disciples. Then they began to go back through the towns where
they had preached. They encouraged the Christians at each
place. At the same time they warned that as Christians they
would have to suffer before reaching God's kingdom in
heaven. They appointed 'elders' in each city, to be what we
would now call priests, as well as to keep the new Christians
together. From Perga, the first town where they had preached
in Pisidia, they went to the port of Attalia. From there they
sailed back to their base at Antioch in Syria, where they
stayed for some time.

Saint Paul (V)
The Council in Jerusalem

It was at this time, around AD 48 or 49, that the famine was severe in Judea. It was also the time when some Jewish Christians from Jerusalem were making trouble among the Christians in Antioch. It seems that Paul and Barnabas were sent to Jerusalem, possibly on two different occasions, first to bring the famine relief money collected in Syria, and soon afterwards to ask for guidance about whether the Christians who had been pagans need keep the Jewish Law.

At the meeting in Jerusalem Peter and James decided that the Greek Christians need not keep the Jewish Law except for one or two practical rules. These were to make it easier for the Jewish and the non-Jewish Christians to eat together. They wrote a letter explaining this for Paul and Barnabas to take back to Antioch. They also sent with them Jude and Silas from the Jerusalem church. All the Antioch Christians met together to read the letter. They were delighted with the encouragement it gave them. Jude and Silas spent some time there, speaking and teaching, before they returned to Jerusalem.

Saint Paul (VI)
In Macedonia

Soon after this, probably in AD 50, Paul said to Barnabas, 'Let us go back and visit all the towns where we preached, so that we can see how our brother Christians there are getting on'. Barnabas wanted to take John Mark with them again but Paul was against it because he felt that Mark had deserted them in Pamphilia on their earlier journey and had refused to share their work. There was a violent quarrel. Barnabas and Mark sailed off to Cyprus. Paul took Silas with him and went by land round into Cilicia, to Derbe and Lystra where he had been before with Barnabas.

The Christians in Lystra and Iconium spoke well of a man there called Timothy, whose mother was Jewish and whose father was Greek. Paul wanted Timothy to join him but, as many of the people there were Jewish, he had him circumcised like a Jew. Then, taking Timothy with them, they went on visiting different towns, telling them of the decisions of the apostles in Jerusalem and the rules they should keep.

They went north through Galatia towards Ancyra (now

called Ankara, the capital of modern Turkey). They had thought to go on to Bithynia, the region along the Black Sea, but the Holy Spirit guided them west instead. They travelled over three hundred miles from Galatia to the sea at Troas, opposite Thessalonica (now Salonica) in Macedonia, in northern Greece. One night while they were at Troas Paul had a vision. He saw a Macedonian appealing to him, 'Come across to Macedonia and help us'.

Saint Luke joined them at Troas and sailed with them to the island of Samothrace, and next day to Neapolis in Thrace, eastern Macedonia. From there they went about twenty miles inland to Philippi, a Roman colony. In these new Roman towns the Jews were not allowed to have a synagogue or to preach publicly. The Jews of Philippi had to meet outside the gates, near the river, for prayers. Paul, with Luke, went there and began to preach. One of the women, called Lydia, a trader in purple dye, was converted and baptised with all her household. She invited Paul with his companions to stay in her house, and she would take no refusal.

There was a slave girl in the town who used to earn a great deal of money for her owners by telling fortunes. She started following Paul and the others as they were going to prayer. She was possessed by a spirit which made her shout, 'Here are the servants of the most high God. They have come to tell you how to be saved.' She did this every day till Paul became upset. He turned and said to the spirit, 'I order you in the name of Jesus Christ to leave the woman'. The spirit left her then and there – and so did her power to tell fortunes.

Her owners, when they found that they could make no more money by her fortune-telling, went and seized Paul and Silas. They dragged them to the law courts in the market place. There they charged them before the magistrates with causing a disturbance and with anti-religious propaganda. The crowd turned against the Christians, so the magistrates had them flogged and imprisoned. Their feet were put in the stocks, bolted and locked.

That night Paul and Silas, happy to suffer as our Lord had done, were praying and singing when an earthquake shook the prison violently. All the doors flew open and the chains fell off the prisoners. The warder in charge woke up with the shock. When he saw all the doors open he drew his sword and was going to kill himself for having let the prisoners escape. But Paul shouted at the top of his voice, 'Don't harm yourself. We are all here.' The warder called for lights. He rushed in and threw himself trembling on the ground in front of the two Christians. When they had calmed him down he led them out of the prison and asked them, 'What must I do to be saved?' 'Believe in the Lord Jesus,' they told him, 'and you will be saved and your family too'. He took them to his quarters in the prison where he got them to tell all his family the good news about our Lord. He washed their wounds and sores, and then, although it was very late at night, he and his family were all baptised. Afterwards they left the prison quarters; he took them to his home where he gave them a meal and his whole household joined in a celebration of their conversion.

When it was daylight the magistrates sent round an order to release the prisoners. The warder told Paul, 'The magistrates have ordered me to release you. Now you are free you can go on your way.' 'What!' said Paul, 'They flog Roman citizens in public, without trial; they throw us into prison. Then they think they can push us out on the quiet! Oh no! They must come themselves and escort us out.' The officers reported this back to the magistrates, who were horrified. They had not realised the men were Roman citizens. They came and begged Paul and Silas to leave the town. So from the prison they went back to Lydia's house where they saw all the Christians again; and after giving them some encouragement they continued their journey through Amphipolis and Apollonia, about fifty miles, to the city of Thessalonika, a big city then as now, with a Jewish synagogue.

Paul, as usual, first introduced himself to the Jews in charge; then on each Sabbath for three weeks he spoke in the synagogue, explaining from the Jewish scripture how the prophets had said that Christ would be killed and would rise again. 'This Christ,' he said, 'is Jesus of whom I am telling you'.

Some of the Jews were convinced and became Christians. Many more of the Greeks – those who had already come to believe in one almighty God – also joined them, and some rich women too. The other Jews were angry. They went to the market place. There they got a gang together to start a riot. They thought Paul and Silas were staying in Jason's house so they went there to drag them out. They only found Jason himself and some other Christians, so they took these off to the city council. They shouted out that Paul and the others had been trying to upset law and order all over the place. They said that they were subversive, speaking against the Emperor and teaching that there is another emperor, Jesus. The city councillors were alarmed at this, but they released Jason and the rest on bail.

The Christians waited till dark, then they sent Paul and Silas away secretly to Beroea, about thirty-five miles further west. At Beroea, now called Verroia, the Jews were more ready to listen to Paul. They welcomed him as a teacher and studied the scriptures every day, checking whether what he said was true. Many of the Jews became believers and were baptised. So too did many of the upper-class pagan Greek women, and some of the men.

When the trouble-makers in Thessalonika heard what was happening in Beroea they went there to start more trouble; so the Christians arranged for Paul to leave at once. A few of them took him to the coast, then round by sea to Athens, leaving Silas and Timothy behind in Beroea. Those who had gone with Paul then went back with instructions to Silas and Timothy to join him as soon as they could.

Saint Paul (VII)
In Athens and Corinth

While Paul was waiting in Athens he had discussions as usual in the synagogue with the Jews, and with other people who believed in God. He also had debates every day in the market place with anyone who was ready to discuss or argue with him. Athens was a big, bad city. It was the place where all the Greek philosophers used to come to teach and debate. The great amusement for the Athenians, and for tourists visiting the city, was to listen to the lectures and arguments at the Areopagus. This was the meeting place for the Council, as well as the chief place for lectures and discussions. Some of those who heard Paul in the market place called him an ignorant parrot, but others said that he seemed to have some startling new ideas; so they took him to the Areopagus to explain them there.

When Paul spoke in the synagogues, any pagans who were there usually believed in one almighty God. In the Areopagus the crowds would be ordinary pagans, believing in many gods, so he spoke to them differently. 'You men of Athens, I see, are very religious,' he began. 'As I walked round admiring your temples and buildings I saw an altar with an inscription on it, "To an unknown God". Well, the God whom I speak about is the one you already worship without knowing it. He is the God who made the world and everything in it. He is the Lord of heaven and earth. He does not make his home in buildings put up by humans. He does not depend on anything our human hands can do for him. No, it is he who gives everything – our life, our breath – to us and to everyone. He created the whole human race. He controls how long each nation shall flourish, how far it shall go. He does this to make us all – every nation – look for him, feel our way towards him until we find him. In fact he is not far from any of us. It is in him we live and move and exist, as one of your own Greek poets, Epimenides, said. And another poet, Aratus, wrote, "We are all his children". Since we are children of God we have no excuse for thinking that he looks like any gold or silver or stone statue designed and carved by man.

'When men did not know better, God overlooked this sort of thing. But now he is telling everyone everywhere to turn away from such things. He has fixed a day when everyone will be judged, and judged fairly. He has appointed the judge and has shown him, proved him to us publicly, by raising him from the dead.'

When Paul spoke about rising from the dead some people burst out laughing. Others said, 'We would like to hear you talk about this again'. Some came to join him and became Christian believers. Among these were Dionysius (or Denis) the Aeropagite, and a woman called Damaris.

After Athens Paul next went to the other big Greek city,

Corinth, about twenty miles away. This will have been in the year AD 50, twenty years after our Lord's death and resurrection. There he met a Jew called Aquila who, with his wife Priscilla or Prisca, had had to leave Italy. A few months earlier the Emperor Claudius had made an edict ordering all Jews to leave Rome.

At this time, in all well-brought-up Jewish families every boy had to be taught a trade, so that when they moved from place to place they would have a way to earn their own living. Aquila was a tent maker and so was Paul, so he stayed with Aquila and they worked together. As in other towns, Paul began to hold discussions every Sabbath in the synagogues, trying to convert Jews and pagans to belief in Christ. After Silas and Timothy arrived from Beroea he preached at first specially to the Jews. Then when the Jews turned against him and started to insult him he took off his cloak and shook it in front of them. 'Your blood be upon your own heads,' he said. 'From now on I can go to the pagans with a clear conscience.' Then he left the synagogue and moved to the house next door which belonged to a Christian. The president of the synagogue, who was called Crispus, became Christian with all his family; so did a great many others living in Corinth. They were all baptised.

Presently Paul sent Timothy back to Thessalonika to make sure that the new Christians there were settled in their faith. After Timothy rejoined him Paul wrote two letters, the second not long after the first, to the Thessalonians, and these letters are now a part of the New Testament.

While he was in Corinth Paul had a vision one night. Our Lord told him, 'I am with you. I have so many people on my side in this city that no one will even attempt to hurt you.' So Paul stayed there preaching the word of God for eighteen months.

After this time of peace, promised in his vision, a number of leading Jews, early in AD 52, got together to attack him. They took him to the court of the Roman pro-counsul. There They charged him with making people worship God in a way which broke the Jewish Law. The Roman authorities at that time allowed the Jews to keep their own laws and customs, but Gallio, the pro-counsul, did not wish to get involved.

Without giving Paul a chance to speak he turned on the accusers. 'Listen, you Jews,' he said 'If this was a police offence or a crime I would certainly hear your case. But if it is a question of words and names and your own Jewish Law then you must deal with it yourselves. I do not intend to decide things like that for you.' He sent them out of the court. Then they all turned on the president of one of the synagogues, a man called Sosthenes, and beat him in front of the court house. Gallio refused to take any notice at all.

Saint Paul (VIII)
In Ephesus, Jerusalem and Ephesus again

Paul stayed some time longer in Corinth. Then he crossed the Aegean Sea to Ephesus. This was a famous town in those days. The temple of Artemis (the Romans called her Diana) was one of the Seven Wonders of the World. It was about thirty miles south of Smyrna (now called Izmir). Priscilla and Aquila went with him and stayed on in Ephesus. Although he was on his way to Jerusalem Paul went to the synagogue to speak to the Jews about Christ. They asked him to stay longer but he refused. 'I will come back another time, God willing', he said. Then he sailed for Caesarea. From there he went up to Jerusalem to greet the senior church before returning to his own base at Antioch in Syria in preparation for another missionary journey.

He began this third missionary journey by visiting places where he had founded churches six or seven years earlier. He went to Antioch in Pisidia, in the middle of what is now Turkey, and on to parts of Galatia, then back through Phrygia and west to Ephesus as he had promised.

Meanwhile another missionary called Apollos had visited Ephesus and preached in the synagogue. Apollos was a Jew from Alexandria. He had a good knowledge of Old Testament scripture. He had been converted, either by John the Baptist or by one of the Baptist's disciples; he had been baptised with John's 'Baptism of Repentance'. He believed that Jesus was the Christ, as John had said; he had learned a great deal about our Lord and his teaching. He was a very good speaker, sincere and earnest. But he had not been baptised 'in the name of the Father and of the Son and of the Holy Spirit' as our Lord had taught; and he had not received the seal of the Holy Spirit in Confirmation. While Apollos had been in Ephesus, Priscilla and Aquila had been able to tell him more of our Lord's teaching, and he was properly baptised and confirmed. They encouraged him to go to Corinth where he became a great leader in the Church.

When Paul reached Ephesus he found about twelve of the Christians there who had been baptised with the baptism of John. Paul explained to them the difference between the two baptisms. When they had understood this they were baptised in our Lord's baptism. Then Paul laid his hands on them in confirmation. At once the Holy Spirit came down on them and they began to speak and to prophesy under the inspiration of the Spirit.

As usual Paul began his work in Ephesus by speaking and discussing in the synagogue, trying first to convert the Jews. He was able to continue this for three months before the opposition hardened. As soon as they began attacking Christian teaching Paul took the Christians out from the synagogue group and began daily discussions in the lecture room of Tyrannus. Jews and pagans both came to him there from all the regions round Ephesus and he worked there for more than two years.

At this time, AD 55 to 57, God worked many miracles through Paul. People used to take handkerchiefs which had touched him and use them to touch and cure other people. Some non-Christian Jews when they saw Paul's miracles tried to use our Lord's name to cure people. A group of seven brothers, the sons of a Jewish chief priest, tried to cast out a devil in this way. They said, 'I command you by the Jesus for whom Paul speaks.' The devil, speaking through the sick man, answered, 'Jesus I recognise; Paul I know; but who are you?' Then the man attacked them, tearing their clothes, knocking them over one after the other, handling them so violently that they ran out of the house badly mauled. The whole city heard about this and spoke about our Lord Jesus with respect.

Some of the new Christians confessed that they had

formerly practised magic. They collected their books of magic, worth altogether something like fifty thousand pounds of our money, and made a public bonfire of them.

Another serious disturbance took place while Paul was in Ephesus. Because of the famous statue of Artemis many tourists and pagans on pilgrimage came to the city. They used to buy silver model shrines of the goddess; there was a whole industry of silversmiths making these shrines. One silversmith called Demetrius employed a large number of craftsmen in the trade. He called a general meeting of the silversmiths' union. 'You know', he said, 'how we depend on this industry for our prosperity. Now you must have seen how this man Paul is persuading many people, not just in the city but all over the province, that gods made by hand are not gods at all. This discredits our trade. It threatens the popularity of our great goddess, Artemis. It could end up by ruining the reputation of a goddess venerated all over the civilised world.' Speaking like this he worked the crowd up to a fury. They started to shout, 'Great is Artemis of the Ephesians'. Soon the whole town was in an uproar. The mob rushed to the theatre, dragging two of Paul's companions with them. Paul wanted to make an appeal to the people but the Christians, and some friends, pagans, who were officials of the state religion, implored him not to venture into the crowds inside. In the theatre there was utter confusion. The crowds were chanting, 'Great is Artemis of the Ephesians.' They kept this up for two hours.

After a long time the town clerk calmed the crowd. 'Citizens of Ephesus,' he said, 'is there anyone alive who does not know that our city is the guardian of the temple of Artemis the Great and of her statue that fell from heaven? Nobody can contradict this. There is no need to get so excited or to do anything rash. These men you have brought here haven't committed any crime or insulted our goddess. If Demetrius and the craftsmen have a proper complaint they can take them to court. If you want to raise any questions about the city you must do it at the city assembly. We could easily be charged with rioting for what has happened today. There was no reason for it at all.' In this way he got the crowd to disperse.

Saint Paul (IX)
Trouble in Corinth and Ankara

While Paul was at Ephesus, early in AD 57, he wrote a long letter to the Christians in Corinth. This is now called the First Letter to the Corinthians because it is the first of the two which were kept and copied, and which we now have in the New Testament. He mentions however, (in Chapter 5, verse 9) an earlier letter still which has been lost. In spite of his having spent more than two years in Corinth several things had gone wrong in the church there. We get some idea of these troubles from his letter, but he felt he had to visit Corinth again; so presently he said goodbye to the Ephesians and went back by land through the towns of Macedonia – Philippi, Thessalonika and Beroea – then south into Greece to Corinth where he took measures to put things right. He spent three months in Greece and intended to go back to Antioch by ship. However, some Jews had planned to ambush him on the way, so he decided instead to go back through Macedonia once more.

Sometime during his journey back from Greece Paul heard that there were again serious troubles in Corinth. He sent one of his companions to try to correct them. Then he wrote a very severe letter – his third to the same church. This letter seems to be reflected in Chapters 10 to 13 of what is now called the Second Letter to the Corinthians in the New Testament. From Chapters 1 to 9 of this letter it seems that the Christians in Corinth had at last overcome or corrected most of the difficulties. Chapters 1 to 9 therefore may actually be the main part of a fourth letter written to Corinth during the years AD 57 and 58.

In Chapter 11 of the letter, as we have it in the New Testament, he gives a long list of beatings, imprisonments and persecutions he had been through up to that time. Clearly he had undergone many more trials than those told by Saint Luke in the Acts of the Apostles; but his chief anxiety was for all the young churches he had founded.

One of these young churches was in Galatia, probably centred in Ancyra (now Ankara). It may have been at this time that he wrote the most severe and worried of all his letters. This is the letter in which he writes about the visit he made to Jerusalem when he took Titus with him. However, in this Letter to the Galatians, he does not mention the Council of Jerusalem or the instructions about food which were sent from the Jerusalem church to Antioch. It is possible that Saint Luke, in the Acts of the Apostles, has confused two of Saint Paul's visits. Some experts think that the Council took place at a meeting later than the one which Paul speaks of to the Galatians.

Paul's longest letter – a letter to the Christians in Rome, whom he hoped to visit before long – is a fuller and more careful discussion of the same subjects as the letter to the Galatians.

Paul's letter to the Philippians was written from prison, during one of the imprisonments not mentioned by Luke. In the circumstances it is a surprisingly cheerful letter. This may be because the church in Philippi was progressing more smoothly than some of the others. It may have been sent from Ephesus between AD 54 and 57.

Saint Paul (X)
To Jerusalem again

When Paul left Corinth in AD 58 he had seven or eight friends travelling with him. On the way Luke and some others joined him. They arranged a meeting in Troas, the port where Luke had joined him for part of his earlier journey. Paul arrived there first. After Luke and the others caught up with him they stayed on there for another week.

They were expecting to leave on a Monday. On the Sunday – Saint Luke calls it the first day of the week, but as the Jews reckoned their days from sunset one day to sunset the next day this may mean on the Saturday evening – they met to celebrate the Eucharist. Paul preached a long sermon that went on till midnight. They were in an upstairs room on the third floor. It was a warm night and all the lamps burning made it warmer. A young man called Eutychus, who was sitting on the ledge of an open window, drowsed off and fell out. He was picked up for dead.

Paul went down and clasped the boy to him. 'Don't worry,' he said, 'There is still life in him.' Then he went upstairs. They finished the celebration and went on talking till daybreak. The boy recovered and the Christians felt greatly encouraged.

Paul then set off for Assos, which was the next port to the south. Luke and the others took ship from Troas and put in to Assos to pick him up. They went on to Mitylene and in three days reached Miletus.

Paul wished to be in Jerusalem in time for Pentecost if possible, so he decided not to call at Ephesus or spend time in the region. Instead he sent word asking the elders of the church in Ephesus to meet him in Miletus. When they arrived he told them that they would not meet again.

'I am on my way to Jerusalem,' he said, 'and I have no idea what will happen to me there. The Holy Spirit, in town after town, has made it clear that I shall meet persecution and imprisonment, but life is not so important provided that when I finish the race I have carried out the mission our Lord Jesus gave me. That mission was to be witness to the Good News of God's grace.'

He went on to remind them how he had lived with them and taught them for three years, never asking them for money or clothes, working with his hands to earn his keep, to show them by his example how to work for one another. He reminded them of Jesus' words, 'There is more happiness in giving than in receiving'. He warned them of heretics who would try to twist and change what he had preached. Then he knelt down with them all and prayed. By now they were all in tears, especially because he said they would not see him again. They put their arms round his neck and kissed him; then they went with him to the ship to see him off.

Saint Luke gives details of this sad journey. They had to change ships twice and then go on by road. At Tyre in Syria they stayed with the Christians for a week, and they kept warning Paul not to go up to Jerusalem. When he left, the Christians went down to the beach and knelt there to pray, as they had done at Miletus. At Ptolemais the party stayed with the Christians there for a day, then went on by road along the coast to Caesarea. There they called on Philip, one of the seven deacons chosen, like Stephen, by the apostles. Philip had four daughters who were prophets. While Paul, with Luke and the others, was staying there, Agabus, who years before had prophesied the famine in Judea, arrived from Judea to meet them.

Agabus too prophesied that Paul would be arrested by the Jews in Jerusalem and handed over to the Romans. He took Paul's girdle and tied up his own hands and feet with it to show what he knew would happen. Everybody begged and implored Paul not to go on, but he said, 'What are you trying to do? Are you trying to weaken me with your tears? I am ready not only to be tied up but to die in Jerusalem for the sake of our Lord Jesus.'

As they could not make him change his mind they said, 'God's will be done'. After this Paul and Luke and their companions packed their things and went on up to Jerusalem. Some of the Christians from Caesarea went with them. They took them to the house of Mnason, a Cypriot who had been one of the earliest to be baptised.

Saint Paul (XI)
In Jerusalem

Next day they called on James and the other senior Christians in the Jerusalem church, who welcomed them and thanked God for the way they had spread the Church through pagan countries. But the Jerusalem leaders had to explain to Paul that thousands of the Jerusalem Christians were converted Jews who still tried to keep all the Jewish Law. 'They have heard', the leaders went on, 'that in those countries you tell the Jews there to break away from the Law of Moses. You allow them not to circumcise their children, not to keep Jewish customs. Now that you are here they will want to have a meeting with you. They are bound to hear that you have come. They may think that you have turned into a false Jew. We would like them to see that you are still a Jew, regularly keeping the Law yourself.

'We have four men here who are under a vow. We suggest you take these men with you and go through the Jewish purification ceremony with them. Pay their expenses. They have to shave their heads and make offerings in the Temple when the time is over. If you do this with them then all our Jewish Christians will know that you still keep the Law and that any rumours about your turning against it are not true. For the pagans who have become Christians, they need only keep the rules we wrote about earlier on. We have no worry about them.'

The following day Paul took the four men and was purified with them. He visited the Temple. He gave notice to the Jewish priests, informing them of the time when the period of purification would finish and when the offerings would have to be made for each of them. He was in the Temple again, before the end of the seven days, when some Jews from one of the places where he had trouble caught sight of him.

Saint Paul (XII)
Arrest

One of the Christians who had come to Jerusalem with Paul was a Greek from Ephesus. He was called Trophimus. The trouble-makers had seen Trophimus in the city with Paul earlier on. They assumed that Paul had brought Trophimus into the 'Holy Place', the inner part of the Temple where only Jews were allowed. They shouted out to the crowds, 'Help, help! Men of Israel! This is the man who preaches to everyone everywhere against us Jews, against the Law and against this Temple. Now he has fouled the Holy Place by bringing pagan Greeks in here with him.' This roused the crowds and made such a disturbance that people came running from every direction. They caught hold of Paul to drag him out of the Temple. They would have killed him, but the Roman garrison commander heard of the rioting and ordered out some companies of soldiers who charged into the crowds. When the Jews saw the commander and the troops they stopped beating Paul. The commander arrested him and had him handcuffed and chained. Then he asked who he was and what he had done. People shouted so much and such different things that the commander could not get any real information, so he ordered him to be taken into the headquarters. The crowd followed, becoming still more violent and shouting, 'Kill him!' In the end the soldiers had to carry him up the steps.

As they were going up the steps into the fortress, Paul asked the commander if he could have a word with him. 'Oh! You speak Greek,' said the commander. 'I thought you were that Egyptian who started the revolt recently. He led four thousand bandits out into the desert.' 'I am a Jew,' said Paul, 'a citizen of Tarsus in Cilicia. Please let me speak to the people.'

The commander agreed, so Paul stood at the top of the steps. When they were a little quieter he spoke to them in Aramaic. 'My brothers and my fathers, let me speak in my defence.' When they realised that he was speaking to them in their own language they became quite quiet. Then he began to tell them how he had first persecuted the Christians; how he had been stopped and converted by our Lord outside Damascus; how Ananias, a very well-respected Jew, had cured his blindness and baptised him. 'Once, when I was back in Jerusalem,' he went on, 'I was praying in the Temple when I fell into a trance. I saw the Lord again. "Hurry!" he said to me, "Leave Jerusalem at once. They will not accept your evidence about me here." "Lord," I answered, "they know that I used to go from synagogue to synagogue imprisoning and flogging those who believe in you. When they killed Stephen I was standing by, encouraging them and minding their clothes." Then he said to me, "Go! I am sending you to the pagans far away."'

When the crowd heard this they began to shout again, 'This man is not fit to live. Get rid of him.' The commander then decided to have Paul questioned in the cruel way they commonly used, beating a man until he answered each question. They took him inside the fortress and strapped him down to a bench; but Paul asked the captain on duty, 'Is it legal to flog a Roman citizen before he has been tried and convicted?' The captain went at once to the commander. 'Do you realise what you are doing?' he said. 'This man is a Roman citizen.' The commander, when he heard this, went and asked Paul if it was true: 'It cost me a great deal of money to get Roman citizenship', he said. 'I was born to it', replied Paul. So the commander decided to keep him safe. The next day he gave orders for a meeting with the chief priests and all the Sanhedrin council, so as to find out what exact charge they had to bring against Paul. Then he brought Paul to the meeting and gave him a chance to speak.

'My brothers,' Paul began, 'to this day I have a clear conscience before God ...' Ananias, the high priest, interrupted, telling one of his people to strike Paul on the mouth. 'Surely God will strike you for this, you whitewashed wall', said Paul. 'How can you sit there to judge me according to Jewish Law when you break the Law yourself, ordering someone to strike me?' The attendants said, 'It is God's high priest you are insulting'. 'I did not realise it was the high priest', replied Paul. 'I should not use such language to one of the rulers.'

When he was able to go on speaking he called out, 'Brothers, I am a Pharisee and the son of Pharisees. It is because we believe in the resurrection of the dead that I am on trial.' This started a dispute between the Pharisees and the Saducees because the Pharisees believed in the resurrection of the dead, and in angels and spirits. The Saducees did not. The two parties began shouting at one another. Some of the Pharisees protested, 'We find nothing wrong with this man. Perhaps some spirit or angel really has spoken to him.' The Saducees then tried to grab Paul. At this the commander ordered his soldiers to go down to bring Paul into the fortress. He was afraid that otherwise they would tear Paul to pieces.

That night Paul had a vision of our Lord saying, 'Courage! You have been my witness in Jerusalem. Now you must do the same in Rome.'

Saint Paul (XIII)
Conspiracy

Meanwhile some of the Jews, about forty of them, formed a conspiracy to kill Paul. They told the chief priests that they must apply to the commander to send Paul down to them again, 'as though you meant to examine his case more closely. We, on our side,' they said, 'are prepared to dispose of him before he reaches you.'

A nephew of Paul heard of this conspiracy. He went to the fortress and told Paul. Paul called one of the officers to take the young man to the commander. The commander, when he had taken him aside and listened to him, let him go but warned him not to let anyone else know that he had spoken to the officers. Then he called two captains and gave them orders to take Paul down to Caesarea with two companies of regular soldiers, seventy cavalry and two hundred irregulars. They left at nine o'clock at night with Paul on horseback, to take him to Felix, the governor of Judea. The commander, whose name was Claudius Lysias, sent a letter with them explaining that since there was no charge against him under Roman law he would tell the Jews to take up their case at the governor's court in Caesarea.

The soldiers escorted Paul by night to Antipatris. Next day the infantry went back to Jerusalem while the cavalry took him on to Caesarea where they delivered him, with Lysias' letter, to Antoninus Felix, the governor. He kept Paul in custody. Five days later Ananias, with some other members of the Sanhedrin, came down to Caesarea, bringing with them a professional barrister to argue their case. Felix arranged for a court hearing. At the hearing Tertullus, the barrister, made a speech saying that Paul created trouble among the Jewish communities everywhere, and that he had brought pagans into the Temple, against Jewish Law. The Jews, he said, wished to try him in Jerusalem but the commander, Lysias, had taken Paul out of their hands. Lysias would be able to confirm all this.

When the governor signed to him to reply Paul said that it was only twelve days since he had reached Jerusalem. In Jerusalem they had not seen him arguing with anyone, nor speaking to the crowds, whether in the Temple, in the synagogues or around the town. The accusations were not true and the accusers could not prove them. He went on to say that as a Pharisee he did believe in the dead rising again, and in the Jewish Law and in all that the prophets had written. He had come to Jerusalem to bring money to help his own people and to give offerings to the Temple. He had done this according to Jewish Law and had caused no disturbance. Some Jews from other places had complained. They were the ones who should have come to Caesarea to make out their case. But Ananias and the Sanhedrin, who were the ones actually accusing him in Caesarea, had been unable, when they examined him in Jerusalem, to find him guilty of any crime. There had been one single outburst when Paul had said he believed in the resurrection and the Pharisees and Saducees began shouting at each other, creating a riot.

Saint Paul (XIV)
Imprisonment in Caesarea, Appeal to Caesar

At this point Felix decided to adjourn the trial until Lysias came down from Jerusalem. He kept Paul under house arrest but allowed his friends to look after him. In the end he kept him in custody for two years, which was the legal limit for a prisoner still on trial. He even left him in custody when he ended his term as governor. He seems to have given the next governor, Festus, some account of what had happened, because Festus also refused to bring Paul to Jerusalem for trial there. On his first visit to Jerusalem he told the chief priests that if they wished to charge Paul with any crime they should go back with him to Caesarea. They did this. The day after Festus got back there he took his seat in court; the Jews from Jerusalem brought many accusations against Paul; but they could not bring proof of any of them.

Festus wished to make a good impression with the Jews at the start of his governorship so he asked Paul if he would be willing to go to Jerusalem for trial. 'No,' replied Paul. 'As a Roman citizen I should be tried in Caesar's court, by Caesar's governor, here in Caesarea. I have done nothing wrong against the Jews, as you know. If I am guilty of a crime under Roman law I do not ask to escape punishment. But if the accusations they make are untrue then no-one has the right to hand me over to them. I appeal to Caesar.'

As a Roman citizen Paul had a right to appeal to Caesar's

court in Rome. Festus knew this. After some discussion he replied, 'You have appealed to Caesar. To Caesar you shall go.'

A few days later King Agrippa and his sister, Berenice, came to Caesarea to pay their respects to the new governor. They were children of Herod Agrippa the First, the Herod who had had James, the brother of John, put to death and who had put Peter in prison. As Agrippa and Berenice were Jews, Festus explained the case to them. King Agrippa was interested; he asked to hear what Paul had to say. The next day Festus arranged a hearing in the Audience Chamber. The King and Berenice attended in state; the Roman commanders and the city officials were all invited.

Festus began by explaining his own position. 'This man', he said, 'is one about whom the Jewish community have petitioned me, both in Jerusalem and here in Caesarea. They maintain that he ought not to be allowed to remain alive. For my part I am satisfied that he has not committed any crime punishable by death; but as he himself has appealed to be tried by the Emperor I have agreed to send him to Rome. When I send him, however, I must write explaining the case to His Majesty the Emperor, and I have nothing definite to say. This is why I have brought him out before you so that I may have something to write. It seems to me pointless to send a prisoner without indicating what the charges are against him. You especially, King Agrippa, will understand the case from the Jewish side; you may be able to help me to explain it.'

King Agrippa then gave Paul an opportunity to speak in his own defence. Luke may have been present. He gives Paul's reply rather fully in the Acts of the Apostles. Paul first explained how he had been a very strict Pharisee, how he had persecuted the Christians, throwing them into prison, voting for their execution and even pursuing them outside Judea and Palestine. He went on to give an account of his conversion on the road to Damascus, of how he had started preaching and how the Jews opposed him. 'So I have stood firm to this day,' he went on, 'saying nothing more than what the prophets, and Moses himself, said would happen. They said that the Christ would suffer; that he would be the first to rise from the dead; that he would proclaim the light

– the light which now shines for our people, and for the pagans too.'

Festus interrupted here. He said that all Paul's learning must be driving him mad. But Paul replied, 'The King understands what I am saying. He knows what Moses and the prophets wrote. King Agrippa, do you believe the prophets? I know you do. You know what Jesus has done. These things were not done in a corner but in public. You can see that they were just as the prophets foretold.'

'A little more,' said King Agrippa, 'and your arguments would make a Christian of me'. 'I wish to God', replied Paul, 'that everyone who has heard me today would become like me – except for these chains'.

Saint Paul (XV)
The Journey to Rome

The King, the governor and the others then went out to talk over the case. They all agreed that Paul had done nothing which deserved death or imprisonment. Agrippa said to Festus, 'He could have been set free if he had not appealed to Caesar'. As it was, the governor felt he had to send Paul as a prisoner to Rome. Paul and some other prisoners were put in charge of a captain called Julius. As it was autumn there were no direct sailings to Rome, so they went on board a ship at Adramyttium, bound for ports in Asia Minor. Luke and some others were with them. They put in to Sidon where Julius allowed Paul to visit his friends, who looked after him. From there the winds were against them so they sailed west along the south coast of Cyprus, then across the open sea to Myra in Lycia, taking two weeks to get there.

There they found an Alexandrian ship from Egypt, bound for Italy, so they were transferred to this ship. The winds were still north or north-westerly. They had great difficulty in reaching Cnidus in Crete; they could not berth there because the wind was against them, so they sailed under the lee of Crete off Cape Salmone and struggled along the coast to a place called Fair Havens, near the town of Lasea. The harbour was unsuitable for wintering, and the guard captain, after discussion with both the captain of the ship and the owner, but against Paul's advice, decided to try for another harbour in Crete called Phoenix which they thought more suitable. But the wind soon changed and gave way to a north-easterly hurricane. It burst on the ship so suddenly that they could not bring it round to face the wind, so they had to run before it. The ship's boat, which they had been towing, was driven forward out of control. As they passed under the small island of Canda they managed to haul it on board. With the help of the ship's tackle they were able to fix cables round the hull. Then they floated out a sea-anchor and let themselves drift.

Next day, as the storm continued, they began to throw out the cargo; and the following day, in desperation they threw the ship's gear overboard. For day after day they could see neither sun nor stars. They went on short rations and gave up hope of surviving. At this time Paul had a vision of an angel who stood by his side. 'Do not be afraid,' the angel said. 'You are going to appear before Caesar. For this reason God grants you the safety of all those who are sailing with you.' Next day Paul told this to the whole ship's company. He urged them not to give up hope. He said they would be stranded on some island.

On the fourteenth night, about midnight, the crew felt that some land was near. They took soundings. As they got into shallow water they threw out four more sheet anchors from the stern to slow the ship. Some of the crew began to lower the ship's boat into the water, pretending they were going to lay out anchors from the bows, but intending actually to abandon the others on board. Paul told the guard captain, 'Unless those men stay on board you cannot hope to be saved'. The soldiers then cut the ropes before the crewmen could climb in, letting the boat drop into the sea empty.

Before daybreak Paul urged them all to have something to eat. He promised that not a hair of their heads would be lost. He blessed bread in front of them and started to eat. They began to be more cheerful. When they had eaten what they wanted they threw the rest of the corn overboard to lighten the ship still more. By now it was almost water-logged.

Saint Paul (XVI)
Malta and Rome

The island where they were shipwrecked was Malta. The local people were very kind to them. They made a great bonfire because the weather was cold and it started to rain. Paul was helping to gather sticks. As he put them on the fire a poisonous snake, brought out by the heat, bit his hand and would not let go. The Maltese, seeing this, and because they realised that Paul was a prisoner, decided that he must be a murderer. Even if he escaped drowning, they said, God would not let him live. But Paul shook the snake off into the fire. They expected him to swell up or drop down dead. When nothing happened to him they changed their minds and said he must be a god.

Publius, the Roman governor of the island, heard of the shipwreck. He took care of Paul and the others for three days. His father was in bed and feverish with dysentery so Paul went in to see him. He prayed, laid hands on him and cured him. Other sick people on the island heard of this. They too came to Paul and he cured them. After staying three months in Malta they went on board another ship from Alexandria which had been sheltering there during the winter. The Maltese, who now had great respect for Paul and the Christians, put plenty of provisions on board for them. Then they sailed for Syracuse in Sicily where they spent three days, then to Rhegium for a day, then with a good south wind to Puteoli (Pozzuoli) in the gulf of Naples in a single day. There were already some Christians there and they stayed a week with them before going on to Rome by land.

The Christians in Rome heard that Paul was coming. They came out as far as the Forum of Appius and the Three Taverns, some 30 or 40 miles, to meet the party. When they arrived in the city Paul was allowed to live in private lodgings with one soldier to guard him. Here he followed his usual custom of speaking first to the leading Jews. At his request, only three days after his arrival they came to see him, and he explained briefly why he was a prisoner and why he had appealed to Caesar.

At this first meeting the Jews said that they did not know anything against Paul although they had heard bad things about Christians generally. They arranged a second meeting, which started early in the morning and lasted all day. As in other places some of them were seriously interested and became believers but most of them refused. In the end Paul quoted the saying of Isaiah, who long before had told the Jewish nation that they had grown coarse; 'their ears are dull of hearing and they have shut their eyes for fear lest they should ... understand and be converted.' 'This salvation of God', Paul told them, 'has been sent to the pagans; they will listen to it.'

Saint Paul (XVII)
Evangelisation from Prison

Paul spent the whole of two years, AD 61 to 63, in his own rented lodging. Although he was a prisoner he was able to receive visitors freely, to spread the kingdom of God and to teach the truth of Christ through those who came to see him. During this time he also wrote letters to Laodicea and Colossae, two cities something over a hundred miles east of Ephesus where he had worked from around AD 55 to 57. His letter to the Colossians is in the New Testament, but the one to Laodicea has been lost – unless it is the one now called the Letter to the Ephesians. The 'Ephesians' letter, unlike Paul's other letters, does not say to whom it is addressed. He also wrote a short letter to a friend of his, Philemon, about a slave who belonged to Philemon and who had been working for Paul. He says in this letter that he is writing it entirely by hand. His other letters he seems normally to have dictated, often adding at the end, in his own handwriting, his name, with some words of encouragement. (His second letter to Thessalonika he ended, 'From me, Paul, these greetings are in my own handwriting. This is the mark of the genuineness of every letter. This is my own writing. May the grace of our Lord Jesus Christ be with you all.')

Saint Paul (XVIII)
Last Years and Martyrdom

AD 53 is as far as Saint Luke's account in the Acts of the Apostles goes. It may have been at this time that Luke wrote his Gospel and the book of Acts. We have no written record for the rest of Paul's life, but we think he was set free after two years' imprisonment in Rome and was able to make at least one more missionary journey before being imprisoned for the last time. During these last years he seems to have sent three more personal letters, one to Titus and two to Timothy. Both Titus and Timothy had been companions and helpers during his earlier missions.

These three letters are sometimes called the Pastoral Epistles because they are mostly concerned with advice and help for the younger men carrying on Paul's work as shepherds – 'pastors' – of Christ's 'flocks', Titus in Crete and Timothy in what is now south-west Turkey. Some heretics in the second century, and a number of scholars in this twentieth century, have thought that these three letters were written many years after Paul's death by someone else claiming to write with Paul's authority. The vocabulary, the words used to express Paul's ideas, are very different from those he regularly used in his earlier letters. They are more like those used in Luke's two books, and are also still more like the words used by Christian writers fifty years later. Perhaps in the earlier letters Paul dictated word for word what he wanted to say and the actual writer took it down quickly and accurately – possibly in shorthand. It may be that in the Pastorals Paul told the writer the gist of what he wanted to say and the friends for whom he wished to include special messages, leaving it to his helper to put it down on papyrus using his own words.

Modern scholars tend to argue that church organisation and ideas must have developed slowly, and that therefore the well organised churches with bishops and deacons, some receiving salaries, with rules of discipline and so on, must belong later than the lifetime of Paul or Timothy. But there is evidence in both Jewish and Christian writings outside the New Testament that both Jewish and Christian ideas and organisations were developing very fast in the years before the fall of Jerusalem, as well as afterwards.

The second letter to Timothy was written from prison again and ends sadly, 'Demas has deserted me ... Crescens has gone to Galatia and Titus to Dalmatia. Only Luke is with me ... Alexander has done me a lot of harm ... The first time I had to defend myself in court there was not a single witness to support me. Every one of them deserted me ... Do your best to come to me before winter ... Eubulus, Pudens, Linus, Claudia and all the brothers send you greetings. The Lord be with your spirit. Grace be with you.'

The letter of Bishop Clement of Rome to Corinth, written sometime between AD 90 and 100, implies that one of Paul's journeys took him as far as Spain. This must have been between Paul's first and second Roman imprisonment. In his second letter to Timothy it is clear that Paul's case had already been heard in court and he foresaw that he would not live long. We know from Clement's letter that both Peter and Paul were killed, almost certainly during the reign of Nero. Saint Peter would have been crucified as this was the regular punishment for 'criminals'. Saint Paul, as a Roman citizen, would have been beheaded with a sword.

Saint Paul (XIX)
The Apostle, his Mission and his Endurance

It was on Peter that our Lord founded his Church; and it is through his successors, the Popes, the Bishops of Rome, that he guides it, gives it a centre of unity and a standard of true teaching. But it is clear that in opening out the Church, from its foundation in Jerusalem to its growth through the pagan world, God used Saint Paul in a role which belonged to no one else. Since their martyrdom the Church has always honoured Saint Peter and Saint Paul together as its joint founders, after Jesus Christ himself. Paul was so often and so clearly guided by the Holy Spirit that he was able to teach with the authority of an apostle, even though he had not been with the apostles when our Lord was teaching them before his crucifixion.

In his letter to the Galatians (2.2-9) Paul says that he privately told Peter, James and John in Jerusalem all that he believed and taught, just to make sure that he was working according to God's will, not deceiving himself. In his letters he sometimes distinguishes between what he thinks himself and what our Lord revealed. 'I should like everyone to be like me', he writes to the Corinthians, to encourage those who could live unmarried to work for our Lord. But he goes on to write, '... and this next is not from me but from the Lord: a wife must not leave her husband ... nor must a husband send his wife away.' Then, two lines later, he gives further advice, 'from me and not from the Lord'.

We too, of course, are always being inspired by the Holy Spirit. As Paul said to the Athenians, 'In him we live and move and exist'. But since we are not so completely united to God as he was, we need to be much more careful to check which of our ideas come from God and which ideas come mixed with other people's or with our own, or even with suggestions from evil spirits. We need, as Paul did, and much more than Paul did, to make sure that what we say or do agrees with what the Church teaches. If we are in doubt we should follow Saint Peter and his successors, the Popes, the Bishops of Rome. Otherwise we may be like the Corinthians or the Galatians who caused Saint Paul such anxiety.

What made him so angry was that some Christians started dividing the churches. Some preferred Apollos and wanted to follow him, not Paul. Others wanted to have a feast at the time of the Eucharist. They brought their own food, but did not share it with the poorer Christians. Some of the Jewish Christians wished to keep all the Old Testament rules about food and to eat apart from the non-Jewish Christians. Even Peter did this for a time. Others began to teach wrong ideas. They thought that by doing this or that they could guarantee their salvation, instead of believing, trusting and obeying our Lord. Some went another way and thought that by baptism they were certainly saved and could now live immoral lives. They lived among immoral pagans and did not really try to live a new life, 'dead to sin', in Christ. Some also seem to have accused Paul of being proud and dictatorial.

It was in answer to people like these that Paul wrote, in AD

58 to the Corinthians, 'boasting' of his weakness and listing all the things he had suffered up to that time: often in prison, five times whipped by the Jews, thirty-nine strokes each time; three times beaten with rods; stoned once and almost killed; three times shipwrecked, once adrift on the open sea for a night and a day; in dangers of every kind, from Jews and gentiles and even Christians; hungry and thirsty, often without sleep; working hard not to be an expense to others; and always worrying about the churches, the men and women he had converted. 'Christ was crucified in weakness. He lives now in the power of God. So if we are weak as he was we shall live in him in the power of God.'

In his letter to the Romans Paul wrote that he hoped to visit Rome 'on his way to Spain'. Clement, the fourth Bishop of Rome (Linus and Cletus, the next ones after Peter, seem to have been martyred in quick succession) knew both Peter and Paul. He was with Paul earlier and Paul mentions him in his letter to the Philippians. When Clement in his turn wrote to the church in Corinth he said, 'Peter underwent heavy troubles, not once or twice but many times. It was in this way that he bore his witness before he left us for his well-earned glory. And Paul ... has become the pattern and example of endurance rewarded. He was imprisoned, chained seven times. He was exiled. He was stoned. He preached in the east and in the west, winning a noble respect for his faith. He taught what is right to all the world. After reaching the furthest limits of the west, and giving his evidence in front of kings and rulers, he passed from this world and was received in holy places. In him we have one of the greatest examples of endurance'.

A Note on Authors and Authority

The prophet Isaiah lived from about 765 to perhaps 690 years before Christ, and his prophecies form Chapters 1–39 of the book of Isaiah in the Old Testament. Chapters 40–55 must have been written a century and a half later, but they seem, since the time they were written, to have shared the authority of the first Isaiah. Other books in the Old Testament also were written by disciples or followers in the name, and with the authority, of Moses or other prophets.

The books in the New Testament seem mainly to have been written by the authors whose names they carry; but some experts who study them carefully have suggested different possibilities. Among these experts have been some who wished to explain away miracles, angels, prophecies – even our Lord's resurrection – and have twisted and distorted the evidence to support their own prejudices. But others have made reasonable suggestions which may be useful even though they may at times seem novel and surprising.

The authority, for example, of Saint Paul's Pastoral Epistles, is still Paul's, even if they were written after his death. The Church has recognised in them how Paul, with his knowledge of our Lord's teaching and with the guidance of the Holy Spirit, in his turn guided the churches he had founded. We accept all the teaching of Scripture but we need to understand it intelligently, recognising that the different books were written at different times in different situations; and we have to use their teaching for our own time and our own situation, with the help of God's Spirit and the teaching authority of God's Church.

A Note on Witnesses and Evidence

The life of our Lord, his miracles and his resurrection, are not ordinary things of the kind we are used to. But they are historical; they are true; we believe them on the evidence of witnesses.

The Holy Spirit within us, if we will listen to him, is one witness helping us to see how the life and teaching of Jesus, the witness of his Church and the writings of the Old and New Testaments all agree in showing us something of the true God and of the true way in which we should live and die so as to come to God. If we are good Catholics we are glad to accept the witness of the Holy Spirit, to believe that God is good and that he has sent us his Son to show us his love.

The Catholic Church, living and growing in different parts of the world, is a living witness to Christ who founded it and to the Holy Spirit who guides it.

However, God gave us understanding and reason so that we can test things for ourselves. We can test in our minds that twelve times twelve is 144. We can test in the laboratory that water is a compound of hydrogen and oxygen. We can often test in the law courts whether a certain criminal really committed the crime that people accuse him of. And we can test historical facts by comparing the evidence of different witnesses. In the books of the New Testament the writers insist again and again that what they are writing is evidence, from trustworthy witnesses, of what our Lord really did and taught and was.

From the time of our Lord's ascension, perhaps for twenty years or so the witness of the Church was almost entirely by word of mouth and by the evident power of the Holy Spirit. The apostles and those who had known our Lord while he walked among them and spoke to them told others of all that had happened. They preached his good news. They taught new Christians what he had taught them. They made collections of his sayings which the new Christians learned and repeated. While the eye-witnesses were there, ready to teach and to answer questions, the only books they used were the Jewish scriptures – the books of the Old Testament and a few other Jewish books.

The letters of Saint Paul – those which were kept and copied – were written between AD 50 and 68 – between twenty and thirty-eight years after our Lord's resurrection and his meeting with Paul outside Damascus. These letters are some of the earliest pieces of written evidence we have of our Lord's life and teaching. The other writings collected in the New Testament were all written within seventy years of the resurrection, while there were still some people alive who could speak from memory about our Lord as they had seen and known him.

At the time of our Lord and for long afterwards paper had not yet been made. Notes and short letters could be written by scratching on wax tablets – boards covered with a thin coating of wax. Long letters and books were written on rolls made either from parchment, dried skins of animals, or from strips of papyrus, a kind of rush which grows in Egypt. The strips were stuck together, longwise and crosswise, then pressed, dried and polished. Papyrus, and parchment too, were very expensive; copies had to be made on fresh rolls, copied by hand each time. These rolls could easily be spoiled. They did not last for ever. Some letters and books however were so interesting and useful that people went on making copies, and copies of copies, up to the time when they could be printed on paper, thousands of copies at a time. Many books, even some interesting and important books, written eighteen or nineteen hundred years ago have now been lost completely or have only been preserved in part. Those which have been preserved, and especially those collected in the New Testament, are our chief historical evidence and witness of what our Lord did and taught.

Historical evidence based on the new Testament is reinforced by other writings of the first century and by archeological finds. It is borne out and confirmed by the teaching tradition through the centuries of the living Church. And it is confirmed again, for those who will receive him, by the testimony of the Holy Spirit in our hearts and minds.

2

Evangelists

Saint James' Letter

We know Saint Paul wrote at least four letters to the Christians in Corinth, but we only have two of them now, although our Second Letter to the Corinthians may have parts of another letter included in it. Other apostles and disciples of our Lord probably wrote a number of letters. Our Lord's cousin, James, the head of the Jerusalem Christians, wrote to the Jewish Christians scattered in the Roman Empire. His letter may have been written as early as AD 48 or 50. Many copies of this letter must have been made and distributed. James' letter, like many of Paul's was written because some of the Christians were quarrelling, and especially because some of the rich ones despised the poor. Among the Jewish Christians those who kept the old Jewish Law as well as believing in our Lord often thought themselves superior. Others even thought that they could be 'saved by faith' without living good lives.

James himself continued to keep all the Jewish Law. He went to the Temple every day to pray. But he also looked after the Christians in Jerusalem and taught them that Jesus is the Christ whom all the Jews expected. Because of this the Pharisees in AD 62 took the opportunity, after the Roman governor, Festus, died and before a new governor arrived, to get him up to the parapet of the temple, throw him over and stone him to death.

Saints Matthew, Mark and Luke

Many people besides the twelve apostles had known our Lord and heard his teaching. In those days, because there were few books, people took more care to remember anything important which they heard. Our Lord's teaching was very important, and also easy to remember. At first the apostles and other disciples who spread Christianity could speak from memory to tell others what our Lord had said and done. They were preaching the Gospel for years before any of our four gospels had been written. Then, after twenty or thirty years, some of them began to write collections of our Lord's sayings and doings so as to keep them on record. One of these collections, a most important one, was made by Saint Matthew, the apostle, perhaps with some help from his friends. Saint Paul's letters to the Thessalonians written probably about AD 51 seem already to use words and expressions from Matthew or from a collection used by Matthew. (So does Saint Clement's letter written to the Corinthians about AD 96).

Some time before AD 135 a bishop of Hierapolis in Syria, called Papias, wrote a book about our Lord. Although the book is lost, some quotations from it have been copied in later books. Papias is thought to have known, and to have been taught by, Saint John, but this is uncertain. It is clear that he spoke to many people who had known some of the apostles personally. He seems in this way to have had good, second-hand, information on what 'Philip or Thomas or James or John or Matthew or any other of the disciples of the Lord' had said. He wrote that 'Matthew collected the sayings [of our Lord] in the "Hebraidi dialecto", and each one [of us] interpreted them as he was able'. Saint Irenaeus, who was born about AD 130, and most other writers since then, have understood Papias to mean that Matthew had written first in Aramaic, though this also is not certain. The Gospel according to Matthew which we have today is in Greek, in a Jewish style, intended especially for Greek-speaking Jews.

Papias may or may not have seen Saint Matthew's Gospel in Greek, as we have it now in the New Testament, but he knew Saint Mark's. (We think this is the same Mark who started travelling with Paul and who is mentioned in Paul's last letter to Timothy.) Papias says that 'Mark became Peter's interpreter. He wrote down accurately, although not in order, all that he remembered of what was said and done by the Lord.' Parts of Mark's Gospel are almost the same, word for word, as the corresponding parts of Matthew's, but Mark's Gospel is written from Peter's point of view. Mark evidently did not find it easy to write in Greek but no doubt he was able to speak it more easily than Peter. The experts agree that it was written in Rome, probably about AD 63.

Many experts think that Matthew, or one of the Jewish Christians who had a copy of Matthew's Hebrew-Aramaic Gospel, carefully rearranged all the 'sayings' which Matthew had recorded, with all the 'doings' recorded by Mark, and other sayings and doings of our Lord which he remembered or heard about. When he had put these in a convenient order to be used in teaching new Christians – especially Jewish Christians – he had them all written out in Greek. This made the Gospel according to Matthew which we now use. Of the four Gospels it has been the one most used for teaching us about our Lord. From the second century until a hundred years or so ago Christian writers assumed that Matthew's Gospel in its finished, Greek version, was the earliest of the four. Experts now have many different theories about its date. There are some who think it was written, perhaps in Aramaic, very early, within about fifteen years of our Lord's ascension.

Saint Luke seems to have been born and brought up as a pagan, but he was with Paul on some of his travels, and also in Rome. He wrote his account of our Lord for pagan Greek Christians. At the beginning of his Gospel he says that several other people had already undertaken something of the kind. He seems to have known at least the Aramaic ('Hebrew') Gospel of Matthew, but in a Greek translation a little different from the final version. He also seems to have used in several places parts of Mark's Gospel. He included, in addition, other stories and parables which Mark and Matthew left out. He probably asked people who had known our Lady to tell him something of our Lord's birth and childhood. Some people think he had even met our Lady and painted her portrait. But like Mark and Matthew he could not copy out all that he could find. It would have taken too long and too many rolls of papyrus.

In the last weeks and months before our Lord was arrested he had warned the disciples about the siege and capture of Jerusalem, forty years before it happened. He warned them that it would be so terrible that it would seem as though the end of the world had come. He then went on to speak about the end of the world and the Last Judgement. Mark's account of what our Lord said seems at one point to confuse the two subjects, the end of Jerusalem and the end of the world. Matthew and Luke sort them out more clearly. Because of this, some people nowadays think that, while Mark's Gospel was written before the siege of AD 70, Luke's and Matthew's (at least the Greek version) were finished afterwards. But Luke's Gospel was followed by his second book, The Acts of the Apostles. This ends at AD 63 or 64, at the end of Paul's first imprisonment in Rome. We think Acts was written at this time since otherwise Luke would hardly have left out any mention of Paul's later travels or his last arrest and martyrdom.

Among the experts there are some who believe that Mark's Gospel was written after Luke's. Their theory is that when Peter and Paul were both in Rome some Christians were using Matthew's Gospel and some were using Luke's. Then Peter, with Mark's help, gave a series of talks using the two Gospels in turn and adding recollections of his own, but leaving out, or only giving brief details of some of the sermons and teaching of Jesus. In this way he showed that the two long Gospels were in fact two books of the same Gospel of our Lord Jesus Christ, one written for those brought up in the Jewish tradition, the other for the converts from paganism, but both telling the same Good News. Mark's Gospel – on this theory – is a sort of summary confirming, with Peter's authority, the main accounts of both Matthew and Luke in a kind of pocket edition. Our Lord's moral teaching was already being passed on by Christian preachers and catechists. When necessary they could quote from the longer scrolls of Matthew's Gospel or Luke's, while Mark's gave a more compact and convenient 'message of salvation' which they could carry with them on their travels. Besides the authority of Peter, it had also some attractive details of Peter's personal recollections left out of the other, longer books. (It is Mark who adds, twice over, that our Lord, when he was teaching us humility, 'put his arms round the children.')

There are different traditions about what happened to these three evangelists after they wrote their gospels. The most definite things we know are that Paul, in his second letter to Timothy, said that 'only Luke is with me', and that Mark's relics are splendidly enshrined in Saint Mark's in Venice. Later traditions about them may well be based on fact, but the experts have been unable to find reliable early records to confirm them.

Saint Peter's Letters

During the 60s Saint Peter wrote a letter from Rome to all the churches in what we call Asia Minor – the parts of Turkey on the Asiatic side of the Bosporus and the Dardanelles. This letter reminds Christians of their faith in Christ and of how they should show this faith in different situations, especially under persecution. At the end he says, 'I write these few words to you through Silvanus'. Silvanus (or Silas) is one of those who worked and travelled with Paul. In Rome both apostles used his help. It may have been Silas who put this letter into good Greek before sending it.

Jude, a brother of James and, like James, a cousin of our Lord, also wrote a short letter warning some Christians, as Paul had done, against false teachers joining the Church and making trouble. 'Remember, my dear friends,' he writes, 'what the apostles of our Lord Jesus Christ told you to expect.'

In the New Testament there is a second letter of Peter which is a little puzzling. It repeats some of Jude's letter. Like Jude, it reminds Christians of 'what was said in the past by the holy prophets, and the commandments of the Lord and Saviour which you were given by the apostles'. We do not know exactly how this letter took shape. It may be that when a short letter from Peter was being copied the writer decided to add some other good teaching. At any rate the Church has found it useful and accepted it as inspired scripture. Probably Jude's letter and parts, at least, of 'II Peter' were written late in the first century.

The Letter to the Hebrews

There is a long and important letter in the New Testament written 'to the Hebrews'. In the personal messages at the end it says, 'I ask you very particularly to pray that I may come back to you soon'; and a few lines later, 'I want you to know that our brother Timothy has been set free ... The Christians of Italy send you greetings.' Timothy had been put in charge of the church at Ephesus by Paul, but he may have been imprisoned when he went to Rome to visit Paul. The Jews ('Hebrews') to whom the letter was written seem to have lived at some earlier time in Jerusalem and to have been thinking of going back there. Much of the letter is to show them that Jesus Christ is the real High Priest and that the old worship of the Temple was only a preparation for Christ's priesthood. The letter uses many of Paul's ideas and is sometimes included as one of his letters. More probably it was written by another of the leading Christians in Rome – perhaps Apollos. Clearly it was written before the destruction of the Temple and city of Jerusalem in AD 70.

Saint John (I)
Revelation

The other five books or letters in the New Testament are all apparently by John, the son of Zebedee and brother of the James whom Herod Agrippa had killed in AD 44. The two brothers and Peter had been fishermen in Galilee. They were with our Lord when he was transfigured and they saw his glory. They were close to him in the garden of Gethsemane when he was in agony before his arrest. When he was dying on the cross Jesus told his mother that John was to be her son and she his mother; and from then until her death and assumption into heaven we think our Lady made her home with John.

After the coming of the Holy Spirit, John at first preached alongside Peter in Jerusalem. They were put in prison together after they cured the lame man by the gate of the Temple. But we do not know where John worked after that until the time when he had the visions which he wrote out in the Apocalypse, the book of Revelation.

Revelation begins with seven letters or messages from our Lord, given to John. 'I was on the island of Patmos', he writes, 'for having preached God's word and witnessed to Jesus. It was the Lord's day and the Spirit possessed me.' The messages, some of encouragement, some of criticism, were to the churches at Ephesus and at six other places north or east of Ephesus, up to a hundred miles away. (Patmos, the little island where John was imprisoned, is in the Aegean sea about sixty miles south west of the city.)

Apollos, before he had understood the full message of Jesus, and then Paul, had built up the church in Ephesus. Later Paul made Timothy the head of the churches in the region. It seems that some time later John took over the responsibility.

After the letters to the seven churches, the book of Revelation is a sort of visionary prophecy of the end of the world. Some of the Old Testament prophets like Ezechiel and Daniel had had visions of this kind. One modern expert believes that Chapters 4 to 11 are a prophetic vision seen by John the Baptist, whom our Lord had called the last and greatest of the prophets; and that from Chapter 12 almost to the end of the book it is a vision, or a series of visions, seen by one of the Baptist's disciples.

In the first chapter of John's Gospel in the New Testament, the Baptist was standing with two of his disciples when Jesus went past. The Baptist stared hard at him and said, 'Look, there is the Lamb of God'. When they heard this the two disciples followed Jesus. One of the two disciples was Andrew, Simon Peter's brother. The other was probably John the son of Zebedee, the 'beloved disciple'. Both will have been disciples of the Baptist before they followed Jesus. It may be that John, the beloved disciple, or one of his helpers, was responsible for adding the visions of the Baptist and his followers to the messages from our Lord to the seven churches. In any case the book gives wonderfully vivid images of the destruction of Jerusalem, of Rome, of all the kingdoms of the earth, of the devil himself, and of the final triumph of the Lamb and the happiness of the martyrs and saints in the new Jerusalem, the kingdom of heaven.

Saint John (II)
The Gospel of John

If Revelation was written by John the son of Zebedee, whether or not he added earlier prophecies to those he was told to write to the seven churches, he would have had no secretary while he was a prisoner on Patmos. This might be the reason for his Greek being very Jewish, rough and awkward. The Gospel of John is easier to read since it was put together by his disciples. They do not refer to him by name. They call him 'the disciple whom Jesus loved'. We think he was already an old man when his disciples decided to write down and arrange in order what they had learned from him. The first half-chapter may have been a hymn which he had composed. They have recorded conversations and discussions which the other evangelists had left out. By the time this gospel was written down, the majority of the Jews, in place after place, had so turned against Jesus and against Christianity that, in this gospel, the word 'Jews' means 'enemies' – almost forgetting that Jesus and his apostles, including the beloved disciple, were all Jews.

In John's Gospel the arguments seem like a long-drawn-out case in a court of law. Jesus repeatedly speaks of the witnesses – the evidence – which support his claims. The writers have chosen six of his miracles as 'signs' to show that God the Father himself is witness to his truth. In the end Jesus was condemned by Pilate, but Pilate knew it was for envy that the Jews were forcing him to give an unjust verdict. He then forced the Jews in turn – the Jews who were all waiting for their Messiah King – to deny their own faith and say 'We have no king save Caesar'. They thought they were condemning Jesus, but in the court of heaven they condemned themselves. They said, 'His blood be upon us and upon our children'.

John, the beloved disciple of our Lord, was greatly loved in turn by his own disciples. He seems during his life to have guided the churches in his charge without laying down rules or using any special authority. But some of the Christians in these churches, as in the churches in Greece and other places, began to develop ideas and theories of their own. They said that our Lord was not a real man of flesh and blood but an appearance only. This wrong teaching – this heresy – separated our Lord and his teaching from ordinary human actions. Later on other heretics tried to separate Jesus from God. They invented a sort of mystic super-God and claimed that they were the only people who knew him: they claimed that they were superior to ordinary Christians and to the ordinary rules of right and wrong. Strangely, they used quotations from Saint John's Gospel to support their ideas.

Saint John (III)
The Epistles of John

Experts nowadays think that John may have died before his Gospel was completed and put in shape as we know it now. They think that the three Epistles of John may have been written by his disciples after his death. The first of these Epistles is not really a letter from one person to others. It is more like a fresh summary of the teaching of his Gospel written to correct the ideas of those who were wilfully misunderstanding it. The Epistle starts, 'What was from the beginning, what we have heard, what we have seen with our own eyes, what we have watched and touched with our hands – the Word who is life ... ' The writer insists that Jesus, the 'Word', the Son of God, was truly man. In the second chapter he tells the Christians to keep the commandments, to stop sinning, 'but if anyone should sin we have an advocate with the Father, Jesus Christ ... who takes our sins away'. The true 'knowledge' of God is to accept what we learned when we were first taught our faith: to live in Jesus Christ and to love one another.

The heretics, those who were distorting our Lord's teaching at this time, were the ones we call 'Gnostics' or *those who know*. They believed that God was beyond the understanding of ordinary Christians, and that only those who had a superior knowledge, which they claimed to possess, could be saved.

The second Epistle is a short letter from 'the Elder' to one of the churches under his care. It repeats the commandment to love one another and again speaks out against the 'many deceivers who refuse to admit that Jesus Christ has come in the flesh' as a true man. It warns the local Christians to have nothing to do with these deceivers.

The third Epistle is another short letter to a friend called Gaius. This man had looked after some missionaries who had been turned away from another church by someone called Diotrephes, 'who seems to enjoy being in charge', and who had been making wicked accusations against the church of John.

It is possible, although many experts think differently, that John himself was still alive and that he was the 'elder' – an old man now – who dictated these last two letters and whose ideas, if not his actual words, were explained in the first Epistle against the deceivers. Later writers seemed to think he died about AD 100.

The last chapter of his Gospel – the one about our Lord, after his resurrection, meeting the apostles by the lake of Galilee and cooking their breakfast – was added, perhaps about this time. In it Jesus indicated the kind of death Peter would die. When Peter asked, 'What about John?' our Lord replied, 'If I want him to stay behind until I come, what is that to you?' A rumour then went round among the Christians that John would not die. However Jesus had not said to Peter 'He will not die', but '*If* I want him to stay behind ...' We can understand this as being written by a disciple after John's death to explain that the rumour was a misunderstanding of our Lord's words. But we can also understand it as a comment – a wry comment – by John at ninety years old or more, gently telling his friends that he was as likely to die as they were.

The same chapter also tells how our Lord three times asked Peter if he loved him, and each time told him to feed his lambs and his sheep. One reason why the chapter was added to the Gospel may have been to remind readers that Jesus had instituted some order and authority in the Church he founded. While John was active his local churches might have managed with only one rule: 'Love one another'. But sooner or later they would have had to recognise in their 'elders', their bishops and priests, the authority which Jesus gave to the apostles and Peter, to keep order in the Church.

When Ignatius of Antioch passed through Ephesus and Smyrna around the year 110 the churches were more organised, each with a bishop and a number of priests. By that time it is unlikely that a bishop would have written as gently as the 'elder' did in the third Epistle of John, saying, 'if I come I shall tell everyone how he has behaved'. The rule of love was still the Law for Christians, but some regular church order had already been established, even in the churches which had been looked after by John.

3

Ignatius and Polycarp

Roman Persecution (I)
Nero, Domitian and Trajan

In the Gospels and the Acts of the Apostles – that is, up to the year AD 63 – it was not really the Roman authorities who were the persecutors of Christ and his followers. Pilate was weak and gave a very unjust verdict at our Lord's trial; but Jesus himself said, 'The one who handed me over to you is more guilty'. Until the time of Nero the real persecutors were Jews, not Romans.

Already by the time of Nero some of the anti-Christian Jews had spread horrible stories about the Christians. Nero became Emperor in AD 55 at the age of seventeen. From when he was twenty-two until he killed himself (AD 70) at the age of thirty-two he was a mad and terrible tyrant. He said that it was the Christians who had started the great fire in Rome in his time. He burned Christians as torches for public entertainments in his palace gardens. He ordered all Christians in the city to be executed, and these included Saint Peter and Saint Paul.

In AD 66 there were revolts of the Jews in Jerusalem and in Alexandria; these started the First Jewish War. In the year 70 Jerusalem was captured and destroyed. The war ended with the siege and capture of Masada, a fortress overlooking the Dead Sea, in AD 73.

The next Roman persecution was under the Emperor

Domitian (AD 81 to 96). In the year 95 he had his cousin executed, the Consul, Flavius Clemens; and he exiled the Consul's wife, Flavia Domitella. He seems to have made a general decree under which many Christians, and Jews as well, were executed or imprisoned. He was also, like Herod the Great ninety years earlier, afraid that a new king, a descendant of King David, would come to rule the world; so he ordered all descendants of David to be killed. It was probably at this time that Saint John was imprisoned on the island of Patmos.

Nerva, Emperor from 96 to 98, was followed by Trajan (AD 98 to 117). From the time of Trajan it was part of the law of the empire that anyone who was seriously accused of being a Christian must be ordered to do reverence to the statues of Caesar and the Roman gods, with incense and wine, and must curse Christ. If he refused he must be executed. This was the law of the empire for the next two hundred years, though it was only from time to time that it was used to put large numbers of Christians to death.

In these times the people in the city of Rome were given free bread and entertainment by the government. Many of them did no work. They loved to watch sword fights and fights with animals in the circus or in the new Colosseum. Criminals were made to fight in these shows. If they would not fight they were killed for sport, either by the gladiators or by the wild beasts. Criminals from other parts of the empire were shipped to Rome to make a show for the crowds to watch, and condemned Christians were often killed in this way.

Saint Ignatius

One important Christian sent to Rome as a criminal was Ignatius, bishop of Antioch. After Peter and Paul had moved their headquarters from Antioch to Rome he was the second head of the church in that important city. He was sent with other prisoners, by sea and land. At the stops on the way he was able to meet the local Christians and to write letters to several different churches. Since Antioch at this time was the second most important Christian centre, several of his letters were preserved.

When the prisoners with their guards reached Smyrna, the bishops of Ephesus and of two other cities, Magnesia and Tralles, came to Smyrna to meet Ignatius. They honoured him because he was on his way to martyrdom, and they offered to take letters back from him to their own churches. From Smyrna he was also able to send a letter ahead to the Christians in Rome. Later in the journey he was held up in Troas. From there he sent letters back to Philadelphia, which he had passed through, and to Smyrna where he had made his earlier stop. He sent an additional personal letter to Polycarp, the bishop of Smyrna. These are the seven letters of which copies have been preserved.

When the prisoners crossed over into Macedonia he was welcomed by the Christians of Philippi. After he left them the Philippian Christians seem to have written to Polycarp asking for copies of Ignatius' letters. A copy of the reply to Philippi from Polycarp in Smyrna has also been preserved.

This group of seven letters of Ignatius and one of Polycarp's all date from about AD 107 or 110, after all the apostles had died. But Ignatius had known Peter and Paul: Polycarp had been taught by John. The letters to Magnesia and Philadelphia show that some of the Jewish Christians still seem to have been more Jewish than Christian. Several of the letters show that many new Christians tried to make out that Jesus was not really God, and that the Son of God was not really a man. Some thought that God just used Jesus for two or three years from his baptism until the Last Supper and then left him before he suffered and died. In each of the cities, except perhaps Rome, we see from the letters that there were divisions and quarrels. Ignatius urges the Christians in each place to follow and obey their bishops loyally and to believe what the bishops taught.

Our Lord had promised to guide the Church. In those days communications were not easy enough for every city to keep in touch with Rome, or for all the churches to meet in a General Council, as they did later; so the Holy Spirit guided the church mainly through the bishops.

In the letters which Ignatius wrote from Smyrna he tried to help the churches to whom he was writing, but he was also worried about quarrels which had been going on in his own church in Antioch. He asked the other churches to pray for Antioch and for Syria. When he reached Troas some friends from Antioch caught up with him to tell him that the trouble there was over, so he asked the churches to send representatives, if they could, all the way east to Antioch to show their friendship and brotherhood with the senior church, and to help keep all the churches in touch.

In all these letters he shows that he is longing to die a martyr. He feels that this is the one sure way to reach heaven and to come to our Lord. It is only in his letter to Rome that he writes nothing about false teaching, or troubles, or being united with the bishop. But he appeals to the Roman Christians with real anxiety not on any account to try to save his life. Some of the Christians in Rome, perhaps through the family of the Flavians, may have been able to get sentences on criminals commuted, or even get them pardoned. Ignatius begs them not to do anything of the kind for him. 'I am longing for death', he writes, 'with all the passion of a lover ... Please leave me to be eaten by the beasts, for it is they who can give me the way to God.' His letters helped many Christians during the Roman persecutions, and through other persecutions down to our own day, to face martyrdom – death for Christ our Lord – with the same love and courage as his.

Polycarp, in his letter to Philippi, wrote, 'I ask every one of you ... to practise the same perfect courage that you have seen with your own eyes in the happy Ignatius and in the other martyrs, Rufus and Zosimus – some of your own people too – besides Paul and the other apostles. Be sure these men did not run their race in vain. They did it with faith and honour. They have reached the place they deserved beside our Lord, whose sufferings they shared. Their hearts were not set on this world of ours. They loved him who died for us and for us was raised up again.'

Saint Polycarp (I)
Flight and Capture

Polycarp had been chosen to be bishop of Smyrna when he was only about thirty-eight or forty years old. He lived to be eighty-six or more. One of the many Christians who learned their faith from him was Irenaeus, born about twenty years after the martyrdom of Ignatius. Many years later, writing about Polycarp, he said that what he had learned from Polycarp as a child was 'part of my soul'. Irenaeus later went to France where he became bishop of Lyons. He also visited Rome. It is from him we know that Pope Telesphorus, the seventh bishop of Rome after Peter, was martyred about AD 137 under the Emperor Hadrian. There are no detailed records of Telesphorus' life. Like many Romans he spoke Greek as well as Latin; his memory has always been honoured in eastern churches as well as in the west. Other bishops of Rome also are said to have been martyred. There were fourteen of them up to the year 200; but apart from Clement and Telesphorus there do not seem to be any reliable records left of their lives or deaths – only a list of names.

Polycarp of Smyrna was martyred too – probably on 23rd February AD 155, more than forty years after Ignatius and nearly twenty years after Telesphorus. He had been bishop all that time and had become loved and respected by many pagans as well as by the Christians. When he died the people of his church wrote an account to the church of Philomelium, two hundred miles to the east. They made copies of their letter to send to other churches also.

Several Christians in Smyrna were put to death by the Roman authorities at this time. Some were scourged with whips till they died. Some were buried alive. Others were tortured in different ways to make them turn against Christ and worship the Roman gods. Some were torn to pieces by animals in the stadium, to entertain the crowds, as Ignatius had been earlier in Rome.

One man called Quintus went around among the Christians getting them to volunteer for martyrdom by giving themselves up to the police, asking to be arrested. But this same man, Quintus, when he was in the arena and saw the lions, lost his courage. When the governor offered him the chance he gave in, took the oath to worship Caesar and burned incense in front of the Roman statue.

Another Christian called Germanicus was so brave in front of the wild beasts that the governor was sorry for him and urged him strongly to save himself. He was young and should have a good life ahead of him. But Germanicus drew the wild animal towards him so as to die more quickly and to meet our Lord sooner in heaven. The crowds were angry because they had hoped he would run away to make the lions chase him. They shouted, 'Down with these infidels! Let's have Polycarp.'

Polycarp, because he was the bishop, wanted to stay in the city and let them arrest him like the other martyrs, but the Christians persuaded him to go to a farm in the country, to stay there quietly and pray for his people. While he was there he had a dream or vision letting him know that he would be burned alive.

The police began a thorough search for him. As they showed no sign of giving up he moved to another hiding place. But the searchers, when they had traced him to the first farm, arrested two young house-boys. They tortured them till one of them told the police where Polycarp's new hiding-place was. Then, on a Friday evening, they got together a squad of men, armed with swords as if they were afraid of a fight. They reached his hideout after he had gone to bed in the attic. His friends told him he could still escape by the back way, but he said, 'God's will be done'. As soon as he heard the police arrive he went down to welcome them. He got the servants to give them food and drink, as much as they wanted. He asked them to allow him an hour for prayer. They agreed. Actually he stood praying for two hours, and as he prayed aloud the others listened to him. They began to feel very sad at having to arrest such a good old man. He prayed for everyone he could remember – everyone he had met in his long life. He prayed for the Catholic Church all over the world. At last it was time to leave, so they put him on a donkey and set off for the city.

The police commissioner (who was yet another man called Herod) came out of the city in a carriage to meet them. He took Polycarp up into the carriage and started urging him to save himself. 'What is the harm', he argued, 'in just saying "Caesar is Lord", and offering incense?' Polycarp did not answer at first, but when the commissioner went on asking him he said, 'No I am not going to do what you advise.'

Then Herod started threatening him, but still he would not give any other answer. At last they pushed him roughly out of the carriage so that he grazed his legs. He did not even turn his head. He just stumped away briskly towards the stadium. The crowds inside were shouting and singing so loud that nobody could make themselves heard, but as he went in the friends who were nearest to him heard a voice telling him, 'Be strong Polycarp. Play the man.'

Saint Polycarp (II)
Trial and Death

Inside the stadium the governor was acting as judge, as well as president of the Games – the horrible entertainment. Polycarp was brought in front of him for trial. At first the crowd did not realise that this old man was anyone special, but the police began to spread the word that Polycarp had been arrested and that the man in front of the governor was the bishop himself. When the crowds learned this they all shouted louder than ever.

'Is this the man they are clamouring for?' asked the governor. 'Yes sir', the officers replied. Then the governor in his turn looked at the bishop and tried again to persuade him to save himself. 'Have some regard for your age', he said. 'Swear an oath "by the luck of Caesar". Own up to making a mistake. Just say "Down with the infidels."'

Polycarp turned to look at the noisy crowd all round the stadium. They were behaving like cruel thugs, and they were pagans, so he said, 'Down with the infidels!' making a big sweep with his hand to show it was the crowd he called infidels, not the Christians.

The governor still did not want to condemn Polycarp so he said, 'Take the oath and I will let you go. Revile your Christ.'

'I have served him eighty-six years,' said Polycarp, 'and he has done me no wrong. He is my king and my saviour. How can I blaspheme him?'

'Swear by the luck of Caesar!' persisted the governor.

'If you still think I am going to swear by Caesar's luck – if you still pretend not to know what I am, let me tell you plainly that I am a Christian. If you wish to know what being a Christian means, then just fix a day and a time for me to come and tell you.'

'Try your arguments on the crowd out there,' retorted the governor.

'It was you with whom I thought it might be worth while discussing it,' Polycarp replied. 'We have been taught to be respectful to the government and their officers. They are in power because God wishes them to be. We can discuss things with you as long as we don't give way on what we believe. But it would be a waste of time to try to argue with a violent crowd.'

'I have wild beasts here,' returned the governor. 'If you don't change your mind I'll have your thrown to the beasts.'

'Well then, order them to be let out,' said Polycarp. 'There is no chance of our giving up our good way of thinking in exchange for a bad one. But it would be a very fine thing for *you* to change over from the bad to the good.'

'If you think so lightly of being torn by wild beasts, I'll have you burned to death,' said the governor.

'The kind of fire you are threatening can't go on burning very long. After a while it will go out. But the fire you don't know about is the fire of the future judgement – the fire of everlasting torment which there will be for those who go against God. Why do you go on wasting time. Bring out whatever you like.'

All this while Polycarp seemed so calm and cheerful that the governor hardly knew what to do. He sent his crier to the middle of the stadium to announce three times, 'Polycarp pleads guilty to being a Christian'.

The whole audience, pagans and Jews together, went wild when they heard this. They shouted that he was the father of the Christians, the teacher of Asia, destroyer of the gods, stopping the sacrifices. They called for the Asiarch, Philip, who was in charge of the games. They shouted for him to order out a lion to fight Polycarp and kill him.

These games – these shows – were run under regular rules, and Philip said the beast-fighting acts had already been closed. Then the crowds called out for Polycarp to be burned; some people ran to get timber and sticks from the workshops or the baths. Some of the Jews were among the leaders. When the heap was ready Polycarp took off his cloak and untied his girdle. He tried to undo his shoes, but he was getting old. The Christians loved to touch him and to help him in every way. For a long time now they had taken turns to do him many little services, even helping him off with his shoes.

There was a stake with iron fastenings so that criminals could be fastened and nailed to it when they were to be burned. The men fixed the iron fastenings round him, but he said, 'Do not nail me. God who gives me strength to face the flames will give me strength also not to flinch, even without my being nailed.' So they tied him instead. Then he looked up to the sky and prayed aloud.

'Lord God almighty,' he prayed, 'bless you for allowing me here and now to become one of your martyrs, to share the cup of suffering of Christ so that I may rise again, body and soul, to everlasting life in the immortality of the Holy Spirit ... Amen.'

Then they lit the fire and it burned with a great blaze at first. But it seemed to billow out around him like a ship's sail blown by the wind, making a kind of hollow space about him. The Christians saw this as a miracle; and the pagans were afraid he would not die. So they ordered one of the dagger-men to stab him to death. (The dagger-men were used in the beast-fighting, as they still are in bull-fights, to finish off an animal who is mortally wounded but does not die at once.)

Some of the Christians were waiting to take Polycarp's body away as a precious relic, but the Jews got Nicetes, the father of the police commissioner, Herod, to apply to the governor not to release the body, 'in case', he said, 'they start worshipping the relic instead of Christ'. The letter to Philomelium points out how ridiculous this idea was. Christians worship Christ, not the martyrs. But they love and honour the martyrs who die for Christ; and they pray that they may share their company in heaven.

Saint Polycarp, the letter says, was the twelfth to die for Christ in Smyrna and the hero of whom they were most proud. The letter ends by asking the church of Philomelium to pass it on to other churches after they have read it.

4

Justin and Irenaeus

Roman Persecution (II)
From Trajan to Marcus Aurelius

The Christians had many enemies who used to spread nasty stories about them. When our Lord first told his followers that they should eat his flesh and drink his blood in Holy Communion some of the Jews said, 'This is horrible. How can anyone accept it?' (John 6.60–61). Many of his disciples went away and stopped following him. The Jews who refused to believe in our Lord remembered this for a long time afterwards.

In the early years when the Christians celebrated the Eucharist they asked all those who were not yet baptised to leave after the readings and the sermon. Only baptised Christians stayed for the Consecration and Communion. They called this part of the Eucharist 'The Mysteries'. The Jews then – or some of them – spread the idea that the Christians held secret magical ceremonies at which they ate human flesh and did other horrible things that outsiders were not allowed to see.

Educated people did not believe this any more than they had believed Nero when he said that the Christians started the great fire in Rome in AD 64, but it helped to give the Christians a bad name among the uneducated. About a hundred years later a Christian writer called Melito said that among all the emperors only Nero and Domitian had really believed that the Christians were bad people. He blamed these two for all the persecutions which followed.

The Emperor Domitian, who died in AD 95, considered Christianity unlawful because Christians would not offer incense or wine to the statues of the emperors or pretend that the emperors were gods. Roman officials too were afraid that people would not obey laws issued by the emperors unless they thought, or at least pretended, that the emperors were gods.

In the legends the Greek and Roman gods did so many wicked things that the Christians said they were devils. This made many of the pagans angry, especially those, like the silversmiths of Ephesus, whose business was connected with their religion. Some of the pagans thought that if the gods did wicked things they should not be blamed for doing the same sort of things themselves. They did not like to think that the Christians were any better than themselves, so they made up slanderous stories about the Christians.

About AD 112 or 113 Pliny, the Roman governor of Bithynia-Pontus (now northern Turkey), wrote to the Emperor Trajan asking how he should treat Christian prisoners. Trajan replied that if they were willing to give up Christianity and curse Christ they need not be punished; it was not necessary to hunt them out. But if someone admitted he was a Christian he must be executed.

The Roman pro-consul of the provinces of Asia (the western part of Turkey today) wrote similarly to the next emperor, Hadrian (AD 117 to 138). Hadrian replied that 'if anyone accuses Christians and proves that they broke the law' the Christians must be punished; but if anyone accuses them, saying bad things about them without proof, then the accuser must be punished. In spite of this it was during the reign of Hadrian that Pope Telesphorus was killed.

The next emperor, Antoninus Pius, was generally moderate and just, yet Saint Polycarp was martyred in his reign. Marcus Aurelius, emperor from AD 161 to 180, is also reckoned a fairly good ruler, besides being a Stoic philosopher; yet in his time Saint Justin was executed about AD 165, the martyrs of Lyons and Vienne were killed in 177, and twelve men and women of Scillium in north Africa (now part of Algeria) were taken to Carthage, tried and executed in 180.

Saint Justin

About the time of Polycarp's martyrdom Christians first began to protest publicly against the bad things people were saying of them. Justin wrote two books or pamphlets to the emperor Antoninus Pius (AD 138 to 161), as well as a longer book called *The Dialogue with Trypho* and some other books which have been lost.

Justin was born in Palestine at Flavia Neapolis (now called Nablus), a new Roman city at Sichem in Samaria. After the first Jewish War the Romans had expelled or killed the Jews of Jerusalem and some other cities. They had then given the places new Roman names and sent Greeks and Romans to live in them. Neapolis was one of these cities and the new people there were made Roman citizens.

Justin was born about AD 100 or 110, probably soon after Saint John, the last of the apostles, had died. He was educated as a philosopher, studying Socrates, Plato and the early Greek philosophers. Plato had written about Socrates and developed his ideas. Justin believed that happiness could be found by learning more about God until he could 'see God' with his soul. He was trying to do this one day, walking on the sea shore and meditating, when he met an old man, a Christian. The two had a long discussion. The old man said that many years before Socrates was born God had already shown us something of himself. The Holy Spirit had told us about him through Moses and the prophets. Then, in the time of Pontius Pilate, God the Son, Jesus Christ, had shown himself to us.

Even before meeting the old man Justin had admired the Christian martyrs for the brave way they faced death. He had realised that the stories told against the Christians were not true. Thinking over all that he had been told, reading what the prophets had written, and seeing how their revelations had been fulfilled and completed in Christ, he became a Christian.

He went on living as a professional philosopher, wearing a philosopher's gown, not a Roman toga. He did not, it seems, become a priest. But he travelled to Ephesus and to Rome, continuing, by public and private discussion and by writing books, to bring more people to know God through Christ.

His first book, written about AD 150, was a letter of nearly eighty pages – a petition to Antoninus Pius and his family and the Roman authorities. In it he showed that Christians did not try to do anything against the government. They were taught to obey the Roman authorities and to live good lives. The stories told against them were untrue. Therefore the emperor and his government were unjust in making laws against the Christians. At the end of this first petition he added a copy of the order of the emperor Hadrian instructing Roman officials to be more reasonable in trials of Christians.

We do not know whether Antoninus actually read Justin's petition. It seems that he did issue an order to the General Assembly of Asia. This order appears to have been rather better than Hadrian's. It said that most of the people who were having Christians brought to trial were themselves irreligious, while the Christians mainly lived good lives and trusted in God. He repeated Hadrian's order that a Christian who was found to have committed a crime must be punished, but if he was not found guilty then the Christian must be set free and the accuser must be punished. Neither Hadrian nor Antoninus, nor the next emperor, Marcus Aurelius, tried to revoke the law which said that Christianity was bad and dangerous. So at some times and in some places Roman officers went on persecuting Christians, killing them in the stadium during the dreadful entertainments, or, if they were Roman citizens, having them executed.

Justin wrote a second petition to the emperor after a particularly unfair trial of Christians by Urbicus, the Prefect of Rome. Urbicus asked a prisoner only one question: 'Are you a Christian?' The prisoner called Ptolemaeus answered, 'Yes'. Urbicus ordered him to be executed. A man called Lucius protested that Ptolemaeus had not done anything wrong. Urbicus immediately ordered Lucius also to be killed. Then a third man spoke up and said that he too was a Christian, so Urbicus had all three of them put to death.

The longest book by Justin – the longest which has not been lost – is his *Dialogue with Trypho the Jew*. In this book Justin wrote in the way Plato had written, repeating more or less, and expanding, a discussion which had actually taken place. It had lasted two days. At the time there were several very clever conjurors or magicians in the Roman Empire who seemed to perform miracles; but there were not many scientific people to test them and to help people distinguish true miracles from conjuring tricks. Because of this Justin did not discuss so much our Lord's miracles. He argued with Trypho mainly from the Old Testament books which Trypho knew well.

The Jews in those days, and Jews today, realise that Moses and the prophets had told them to expect a Messiah, a Christ, a Saviour who was to come. But they found it difficult to believe that a man who had been hated by the chief priests and the Jewish leaders – a man executed as a common criminal by the Romans – could possibly be the Christ they were expecting. Trypho felt that crucifixion was such a horrible death it showed that Jesus was under God's curse.

Justin seemed to know much of the Old Testament by heart. He quoted long passages from book after book showing how Christ was to come as a poor man, to be king of a spiritual kingdom. Christ was to suffer and be despised. He was to be killed as a criminal, and then rise again. His kingdom was to start among the Jews and was to spread out among the peoples of the world. He was to come again in glory at the last day at the end of the world.

Trypho raised objections here and there, but the strength of Justin's arguments, one after another, was so great that at the end of the second day Trypho went away to check on Justin's quotations and to think over whether Jesus really was the Christ. We do not know whether he became a Christian.

As a philosopher Justin believed that the great Greek philosophers had learned and taught much which was true about God and how we should live. However he thought that they had learned all this, directly or indirectly, through the Jews and from the teachings of Moses and the prophets.

One philosopher called Crescens had public debates with Justin in Rome. He seems to have come to hate Justin. Because of this Justin expected that in the end Crescens or some other enemies would try to have him tortured or killed. Eventually he was arrested and tried, along with six other Christians, by the Prefect Rusticus. We have a record of this trial; and this is how it ends:

Rusticus: Come up, all of you, and sacrifice to the gods.
Justin: No one in his senses would give up a good religion for a bad one.
Rusticus: If you don't obey you will be tortured mercilessly.
Justin: That is what we wish – to be tortured for our Lord Jesus Christ and in that way to be saved. That will bring us salvation. That will give us confidence when we come to the more terrible trial – the trial of the whole universe by our Lord and Saviour.
Christians: Do what you wish. We are Christians and we do not sacrifice to idols.
Rusticus: (reading from a set form): Those who refuse to sacrifice to the gods and to obey the emperor shall be scourged and executed by beheading according to the laws.

The martyrs prayed, giving glory to God, then went back to prison and were beheaded.

The Martyrs of Lyons and Vienne

In these years, although it was illegal to be a Christian, persecution was not general or continuous through all the provinces of the Roman Empire. That came later. Some officers, like Urbicus in Rome, decided to use the law to torture or kill some Christians. Some people, like Crescens, used the law out of jealousy and spite to have some Christians killed. A hundred years after Justin's martyrdom a Roman officer called Marinus, at Caesarea in Palestine, was being promoted to be a centurion when a jealous rival denounced him as a Christian. Marinus admitted it and was martyred for it. Sometimes the common people, especially the crowds in the big sports arenas, became wild and violent. When rumours went round about Christians being cannibals or having horrible love feasts the crowds would sometimes hunt them out. They enjoyed having a public trial and seeing Christians torn by lions or burned in iron chairs.

Justin and Irenaeus 79

In AD 177, about ten years after Saint Justin was martyred in Rome, there were anti-Christian riots in Lugdunum – now Lyons – which was the capital of one of the most important Roman provinces and the biggest city in Gaul. A number of Christians were arrested in Lyons itself and in the city of Vienne, twenty miles to the south. Several of these Christians had come from Phrygia in the middle of what is now Turkey, or from Pergamum, near Troas, the port used by Saint Paul when he travelled between Asia and Macedonia. After the martyrdoms the other Christians in Lyons wrote a long letter to the churches in Phrygia and other places in Asia where some of the martyrs had been born.

Violent crowds, they wrote, had gone round shouting, throwing stones, breaking into Christian houses, looting, and dragging people off to prison. The Roman tribune, the chief of police, had them pulled out into the market place to be charged in front of the crowd. He then had them locked up again to wait for a big trial in front of the governor. When the governor arrived he began to torture the prisoners as part of the trial. One Christian called Vettius, an important citizen of Lyons, was not on trial, but he could not endure to see the other Christians being treated so unfairly. He went to the governor and demanded to be allowed to speak in their defence. He said the Christians did not commit the crimes they were charged with. Although he was well known and respected, the crowd shouted out against him. The governor refused to let him speak for the defence. He asked him, 'Are you a Christian?' Vettius answered, 'Yes, I am', and the governor ordered him to be taken away with the rest for trial the next day.

When the Christians were back in prison some of them began to lose courage. This made the others very anxious. More Christians were imprisoned, day after day for several days. Some of their servants who were not Christians were rounded up with them. These servants were terrified that they too might be tortured, so they invented stories of crimes which they said the Christians had committed. Some of the Christians were tortured many times during several days. Among these were Sanctus, a deacon of the church of Vienne, Maturus who had only been Christian for a short time, Attalus who came from Pergamum in Asia, and a servant girl called Blandina. Attalus was hung over a fire in an iron chair. When they said that the Christians were cannibals he said, 'What you are doing to me is all but eating me. Christians do not eat men or do anything wicked.'

Blandina's mistress, who was among the Christians in prison, was afraid that the girl would be so frightened that she would agree to sacrifice to the gods, but in the end it was Blandina who seemed the bravest of all. She saw all the others tortured and killed. She was tortured horribly herself. Between the tortures the officers kept questioning her, but she only answered, 'I am a Christian. Nothing wicked happens among us.' She was whipped, mauled by wild animals, burned with fire, and then thrown into a net and rolled in front of a bull. The bull tossed her again and again till at last she gave up her life for Christ. Even the pagans said they had never known a woman endure so many and so great sufferings.

Those who at first had been frightened into saying that they were not Christians were still kept in prison by the police; and the prayers and example of the braver ones gave most of them the courage to change their evidence and say boldly that they were Christians too.

The trial dragged on for a long time because the governor had written to the emperor for advice. The answer, when it came, said, 'Those who will not sacrifice to the gods must be beaten to death. If any of them will deny that they are Christians they should be set free.' In fact some of them, especially of the younger ones, had died already under torture in prison. The youngest, Ponticus, was a boy of fifteen. Most were strangled. A Phyrgian doctor called Alexander may have been a Roman citizen; he was beheaded. The bishop, Pothinus, was over ninety years old and very sick. He was scarcely able to breathe, but was very strong in spirit and longing for martyrdom. When they asked him, 'Who is the God, of the Christians?' he answered, 'If you are worthy you will know'. He died after two days in prison.

The Roman authorities left the bodies of the martyrs exposed for six days as a warning, but the other Christians, those who had not been imprisoned and killed, wanted to take the bodies away to bury them. The authorities set a guard over them to prevent this. Eventually they burned all the remains, throwing the bones and ashes into the river Rhone.

About this time a Greek philosopher, Athenagoras of Athens, wrote to the emperors, Marcus Aurelius and Commodus, a *Supplication for the Christians*. This was very calmly and reasonably written, showing up the lies told about Christians and explaining clearly and sensibly how they were good, obedient citizens of the empire. He begged for them to be given just treatment.

Athenagoras also wrote a little book on *The Resurrection of the Dead*. In it he tried to prove the truths of Christianity from philosophy. He wrote very clearly about each of the three Persons of the Blessed Trinity, about the angels, about celibacy and marriage, and against abortion. He must have been an excellent Christian but we know hardly anything about his life.

Saint Irenaeus

Irenaeus, a priest in Lyons, was one of those who had come there from Asia. He had learned about Christ from Bishop Polycarp of Smyrna who, in turn, had learned from Saint John, the beloved disciple. Several times in his writings Irenaeus speaks with affection of Polycarp and of what Polycarp told him at first hand of John, and at second hand of our Lord.

In AD 177 the church in Lyons sent Irenaeus to Pope Eleutherius in Rome. In the letter of introduction which they gave him to take to the Pope they wrote: 'We have asked our brother and companion Irenaeus to bring this letter to you. We beg you to value him because he is devoted to the covenant of Christ.' Irenaeus may have been on this journey just at the time of the martyrdom of Bishop Pothinus and the others. He was chosen to be the next bishop of Lyons and he worked in France (Gaul) for another twenty or twenty-five years. During that time he wrote several books and letters which later writers have used to show how the truth about God, about Christ, about the Holy Spirit, has continued to be passed down in the Church from generation to generation. Only two of his books have been preserved complete, but both of these are important.

The Proof of the Apostolic Teaching is a shorter book. Like Saint Justin he has used Old Testament prophecies rather than miracles for his evidence. He shows how the whole of the Old Testament is God's preparation for our Lord, for the redemption, and for the beginning of the Christian Church. He quotes from all four Gospels and from almost every book of the New Testament in a way which shows how the Church was coming to accept all these books as Scripture – as truth.

His longer book he called 'The Refutation of the so-called "Knowledge"', but we usually call it *Against Heresies*. The heretics he wrote against are some of those we call 'Gnostics' – those who claimed they had superior 'knowledge', and who made such bad use of Saint John's Gospel. In Saint John's time already some of the Christians tried to make out that they had deeper knowledge about God, beyond what the apostles had taught. As Christianity spread, other people with strange ideas joined them. They imagined another God beyond God, another heaven beyond heaven. They tried to argue that evil came from one god – or from a 'mistake' of a god – and that the good God, the super-God, was out of touch, except to themselves and their followers who had the inner 'knowledge'.

Irenaeus seems to have read all their complicated books and arguments. He shows, one by one, where each had gone wrong. He shows how the truth of Christ and his Church comes to us through the apostles and through the bishops in succession from the apostles. Just as Irenaeus learned the truth of Christ from Polycarp, who learned it from John, who learned it from Jesus, so other churches learn it in the same way from earlier bishops who learned it from the apostles, and especially, wrote Irenaeus, from 'the very great, the very ancient, the universally known church founded and organised at Rome by the two most glorious apostles, Peter and Paul. This is the faith preached to men – the faith which comes down to our time through the successions of the bishops. It is necessary for every church to agree with this church because of its more powerful authority. "Every church" means those people everywhere who are the faithful. In this church always, by people everywhere, is preserved what has been handed down from the apostles.'

During the times of persecution the Holy Spirit guided the different churches so that they kept the same faith and passed on the same teaching, even when it was difficult to keep in touch with the church of Rome. Naturally different customs grew up in different places. Different churches used different ways to select the date for Easter. They had different days for fasting before Easter. Pope Victor (AD 189 to 199) seems to have been the first Pope to try to bring all the churches into line on this. He even threatened to excommunicate some eastern churches who wished to keep their own customs. Saint Irenaeus sent him a letter urging him not to be too strict.

'Some think,' he wrote, 'they are bound to fast one day, some two days, others more than two, others as much as forty. Yet they have all lived at peace with one another.' Irenaeus gives examples of six holy bishops of Rome between AD 115 and 166 who 'sent the Eucharist to other dioceses which did not follow the Roman custom. And when the blessed Polycarp was staying in Rome in the time of Pope Anicetus [155 to 166] they disagreed about some things but were quite friendly and unwilling to quarrel about this. Anicetus could not persuade Polycarp to change his custom. Polycarp said it was what had been followed by John and some other apostles. Polycarp did not manage to persuade Anicetus to change. Anicetus maintained that he was bound to keep to the custom of the bishops before him. Yet Anicetus showed his respect for Polycarp. He allowed him the first place in the celebration of the Eucharist. They parted at peace with each other and kept peace in the whole Church.'

This letter was written 'in the name of those brothers and sisters over whom [Irenaeus] ruled throughout Gaul'. It seems from this that he was what we would now call a 'metropolitan archbishop' for the whole of France. He may have acted as president of a conference of bishops from all parts of Gaul. He was an important link between the churches of John and Peter, of Asia and Europe, of Greeks and Latins.

The Martyrs of Scillium

The oldest record we have of Christianity in the African provinces west of Egypt, and one of the oldest Christian records in Latin, is the official report of the trial and condemnation by the pro-consul in Carthage of a group of Christians from Scillium in Numidia (now in Algeria). Twelve of them were beheaded on 17th July AD 180. In those days north Africa was more fertile than now and formed a highly civilised part of the Roman Empire. It soon became important in the history of the Christian Church.

5

Perpetua and her Companions

Roman Persecution (III)
Septimius Severus

In AD 202 Emperor Septimius Severus made a new decree against the Christians. In different parts of the empire the governors acted on it in different ways. In some places their aim seems to have been to terrify new Christian converts so as to frighten off others who might be attracted to Christianity. In Carthage, after the death of the pro-consul Minucius Timinian, the procurator, Hilarian, was acting as pro-consul. Early in 203 he had a group of Christians arrested, including Perpetua who belonged to the important family of the Vibii. With her he arrested two of her servants, Felicity and Revocatus, and two other men called Secundulus and Saturninus. An older Christian, Saturus, who may have been a priest or a reader, seems to have been instructing the others for baptism. He joined them later in prison and shared their martyrdom.

Saint Perpetua (I)
Arrest

At first they were put under house arrest. While they were waiting for their trial Perpetua and Saturus wrote accounts of what was happening to them and the graces God gave them.

Perpetua was much troubled on account of her father. He kept urging her to give up Christianity and save herself. 'Father,' she replied, 'You see this jar?' 'Yes,' he said. 'Can it be called anything else than what it is?' He answered, 'No.' 'So can I call myself anything else than what I am – a Christian?' Her father was so angry he threatened to tear her eyes out, but he could not do it; he scolded her furiously and went away. He stayed away for a few days, and during that time the group were all baptised.

Saint Perpetua (II)
Prison

They were put in prison a few days later and were very roughly treated there by the soldiers. Perpetua suffered especially from the darkness and the heat, because the prisoners were all crowded together. But she suffered most from worry. She was a young wife, aged twenty-two, with a baby son still needing his mother's milk.

Two deacons of the church paid money to the prison guards to have them all allowed out into a more open part of the prison where they could meet their families. There Perpetua was able to nurse the baby and to arrange with her mother and her brother that the child should stay with her while she was in prison, and that they would look after him after she was killed. 'From that time', she wrote, 'the prison suddenly became a palace for me.'

Her brother then suggested to her that as she was suffering for Christ she might ask God to show her whether they were to be martyred or released. Accordingly she prayed for this and God showed her a vision. 'I saw a bronze ladder', she wrote, 'reaching up to heaven, very narrow, with swords and spears, hooks and knives fixed alongside, so that anyone on it must keep going up, otherwise his flesh would be torn on the iron. At the bottom lay a great dragon to frighten off those who would go up. First Saturus went up. When he got to the top he turned round and said, 'Perpetua, I am waiting for you. Be careful so that the dragon doesn't bite you'. So I said, 'In the name of Jesus Christ, it shall not hurt me'. Then it put its head gently forward as though it was afraid of me; and I trod on its head like a first step. I went on up, and there I saw a great sort of garden with a man in white, dressed like a shepherd, tall, sitting and milking his sheep. Around him there were thousands standing, dressed in white. He raised his head to look at me and said, "Welcome, child". Then he called me and gave me a little of the curd he had by him. I took it in both hands and ate it up. Then everyone said, "Amen". and I woke up, still with a strange sweet taste in my mouth.'

She told her brother at once that they were to die, and they realised that they need not hope for anything else in this world.

Saint Perpetua (III)
Trial

A few days later they heard that the trial was being arranged. Perpetua's father came again. He begged her piteously for his sake, for her mother's sake, for the baby's sake, not to go on to her martyrdom. He was the only one of her relations who would not see that martyrdom was really something glorious; yet he loved and admired her. He kissed her hands. He knelt at her feet. He called her 'Lady'. To comfort him she said, 'We are all in God's power. What happens at the trial will be what God pleases.' So at last he went away, very sad.

Another day, while they were eating, the soldiers suddenly took them off to the forum for trial. Her father was waiting for her there and begged her again, 'Spare my grey hair; spare your little child. Offer a sacrifice for the emperors.' She answered, 'I will not sacrifice to false gods'.

Then Hilarian, the judge, questioned her. 'Are you a Christian?' 'Yes, I am a Christian,' she replied. Her father came and stood beside her to argue again, but Hilarian ordered the soldiers to drive him off, and they struck him with their sticks. Perpetua felt as though they were hitting her, she was so sorry for her father's unhappiness.

Hilarian sentenced them to be thrown to the beasts. They were taken back to prison, to wait for the games at the festival of one of the Caesars.

Saint Perpetua (IV)
Dinocrates

A few days later, while they were all praying, Perpetua suddenly remembered her young brother, Dinocrates, and saw him in a vision. He had been dead some time. He had died of horrible ulcers when he was only seven. She saw him and others coming out of a dark place, hot and thirsty, dirty and pale. He was trying to drink from a great basin of water, but the edge was too high for him to reach it. When she woke Perpetua knew that he must be in Purgatory but she felt sure she could help him by her prayers. She prayed for him every day until they were moved to cages near the camp where the festival games were going to be held.

There, one day when they were tied up, she saw another vision of the place where she had seen her brother. This time Dinocrates was well, clean and happy. The great basin seemed lower and in easy reach. On the edge was a golden cup. The boy came up and drank as much as he wished from the cup. Then he went away to play like any happy child; so Perpetua woke knowing that her brother had passed through Purgatory and had reached heaven.

At this time Pudens, the officer in charge of the camp prison, so admired the courage of the Christians that he allowed their friends to come to see them. Perpetua's father came again, which made her very sad.

Saint Perpetua (V)
Saint Pomponius

The day before the games she had another vision; this time she saw Pomponius who had already died in the persecution. He said to her, 'We are waiting for you, Perpetua'. Then he took her by the hand and led her to the amphitheatre. 'Don't be afraid,' he said, 'we are here to help you'. Then, in her vision, she saw herself as a gladiator fighting a horrible Egyptian and defeating him. After her victory she went up to the master of the gladiators to receive her prize. He kissed her and said, 'Peace be with you, daughter'. So she walked through the amphitheatre to the gate called the Gate of Life. There she woke up, knowing that it was the devil she would have to fight. She wrote all this down, the day before the games; then she added, 'Let someone else write what happens at the games tomorrow'.

Saint Saturus' Vision

Saturus also had a vision which he wrote down. He saw himself with Perpetua being carried by four angels, though the angels did not actually touch them, up a gentle hill to a lovely pleasure garden full of flowers. There they found three friends who had been burned alive earlier in the same persecution, and another friend, Quintus, who had died in prison. They all went forward to a beautiful city like that described in Saint John's book of Revelation. They were taken to meet the Lord on his throne. They were lifted up to kiss him. Then they gave the kiss of peace to all the saints and went out.

On their way out they saw Optatus, the bishop, on one side and Aspasius, a priest and teacher, on the other. Both were unhappy. They went down on their knees to the martyrs and begged. 'Make peace between us. You have gone away and left us like this.' Saturus and Perpetua were shocked. They made them get up so that they could greet them properly. 'You are our father,' they said to Optatus, 'and you, a priest,' to Aspasius. 'You should not kneel to us.' Perpetua began to talk to them in Greek. While they were speaking the angels told Optatus and Aspasius to stop quarrelling. To Optatus they said that he must correct his people. 'They come to you like fans coming home after the match, quarrelling about the different teams.' Then it seemed to Saturus that the angels wished to shut the gates. 'And we began to meet many Christians and martyrs there,' he wrote, 'and we were all refreshed with an odour which I cannot describe. Then I woke up with joy.'

Saint Felicity

Of the others in the group, Secundulus seems to have been killed in prison before the games. Felicity was expecting a baby. Under Roman law a pregnant woman was not executed until after her child was born. She was afraid that her friends would all be killed at the feast of Caesar and that she would be held back for some later games. If that happened she would have to wait in prison, not with good Christian friends, but with strangers and criminals, and be killed along with them. The other martyrs were sad for her. They did not want to leave her behind so they all prayed together. Almost at once she began to feel pains and her baby was born a month before she was expected.

Saint Perpetua (VI)
The Games

The tribune, the officer in charge of the prisoners, was superstitious. He was afraid that the Christians might use magic to help the martyrs escape. This made him torture them; he hated to see them cheerful; but Perpetua went up to him. 'Why do you not allow us to be cheerful?' she demanded. 'We are noble victims. We are to fight in Caesar's honour on Caesar's festival day. You should let us eat well and enjoy ourselves or you will bring shame on the celebration.' The tribune blushed and ordered the guards to treat the prisoners better. The assistant governor of the prison was so moved that he became a Christian.

It was the custom, on the day before the fight, to allow those condemned to death to eat a good last meal. When the warders and others came to watch them Saturus turned to them. 'You watch us enjoying ourselves today,' he said, 'and tomorrow you will enjoy watching us die. You are our friends today and our enemies tomorrow. But our Lord is your judge as well as ours. You will see how we go gladly to our suffering.' This astonished those who were standing round and some of them afterwards became Christians.

Next morning they all went cheerfully together to the stadium. At the gate the guards tried to dress them up as priests of Saturn and priestesses of Ceres, but Perpetua would not allow it. 'We are giving our lives for freedom from those gods. We agreed with you that we would obey you willingly on condition that we should not have to do anything like this.' The tribune gave in and allowed them to go on in their own clothes.

They entered the stadium and went to the front of Hilarian's box. 'You judge us,' they told him, 'but God judges you.' They spoke to the people, warning them to leave their devilish gods and turn to the true God, to Christ. At this the crowd grew angry. They called for the Christians to be whipped before the fighting. After the whipping the martyrs were taken out again to be brought in by ones and twos.

First Saturninus and Revocatus had to fight a leopard; then Saturninus was set up on a raised platform and torn by a bear. Saturus was tied by a gladiator onto the back of a wild boar, but the boar attacked and wounded the gladiator so severely that he died later. Next Saturus was tied in his turn onto the raised platform, but the bear refused to come out of his den.

After this the two women were stripped and had nets thrown over them. They were driven into the arena and a savage cow was sent against them. This was quite irregular and the crowds were horrified to see two young women treated like this; so they were called back and dressed in some sort of clothes. When they went in again Perpetua was knocked down by the cow, her clothes partly torn and her hair dishevelled. She picked herself up, pulled her clothes round her and tried to pin up her hair. Next the cow threw Felicity, and Perpetua went to help her up. The crowds were quieter now, so Felicity and Perpetua were called back to one of the gates (the gate called 'the Gate of Life' which she had seen in her vision). Rusticus, a catechumen, was there and spoke to her. She seemed to wake up from a sleep or a vision and asked, 'When are we going to be thrown to the cow?' Rusticus told her she already had been. He showed her the bruises and cuts on her body and the dirt and tears in her clothes. Then she called her brother. She told them always to love one another, always to be true to Christ, and not to be worried about her martyrdom.

At another gate Saturus spoke to Pudens, the guard there. 'I haven't been hurt at all by the wild beasts yet,' he told him. 'I said all along that I would die from a single bite of the leopard.' At the end of the games the leopard was unleashed against him and did give him one deadly bite. He bled so freely that the Christians said he was being baptised again with blood. 'Well washed!' they called out as he stumbled back to the gate. He reached Pudens and said, 'Good-bye. Remember your faith. Remember me and don't let these things trouble you. Let them make you strong.' He reached for Pudens' hand, took off a ring, dipped it in his blood and gave it back. Then he collapsed. The guards put him with the other dying martyrs where all their throats were to be cut to make sure they were dead.

Then the crowds shouted to have them brought back into the arena and pierced to death in front of everyone. The martyrs – those who still could – stood up to give one another the sign of peace. Those who could not move were killed with the sword. Saturus had already died. Perpetua was pierced awkwardly. This time she felt the pain and shrieked aloud. The man with the sword wavered because he was untrained. She herself guided the sword to her neck so that next time he struck properly and she died. In this way all that group of martyrs followed Saturus to heaven as they had foreseen in their vision and through their faith.

6

Tertullian and Origen

Tertullian

The writer who finished the story of Perpetua and Saturus was probably Tertullian. He was one of the earliest Christians to write books in Latin.

Tertullian was the son of a centurion, a captain in the Roman army. He was born about AD 155. He lived in Carthage and was trained as a lawyer. About AD 193 he became a Christian. From that time he began to write books about Christian subjects. He was probably not the first writer to use the word 'Trinity' for the mystery of the Father, the Son and the Holy Spirit all being one God, but he seems to have been the first to use the word 'Person' for each of the three Persons of the Trinity. He spelled out, what all Christians believe, that we recognise a 'distinction' of three Persons but no 'division' in the one God. Later writers down to today have used Tertullian's books to study and understand our Lord's teaching better.

Perhaps because he had lived an evil life for a time before his baptism he felt he should live a very strict, harsh life of penance afterwards. But, unlike most saints, he wanted all other Christians to live a harsh life too. He admired the heroism of the martyrs and seemed to feel that every Christian should suffer like a martyr. He thought that a Christian who was widowed should never marry again. He thought the theatre and most other kinds of amusement were sinful. He began to follow the ideas of a heretic called Montanus. He made exact rules of conduct. He wished women to cover their heads and faces. At last, about AD 212, he left the Catholic Church altogether and spent his last eight or ten years as a sour heretic.

Clement of Alexandria

A Greek called Clement, born about the same time as Tertullian or a little earlier, was another Christian writer. He believed that the Greek philosophers, whom he admired, had borrowed much of their inspiration from the Jewish Old Testament writings. His own books showed how he saw Christianity and our Lord's teaching as being in harmony with Plato and the Stoics. These books were of some importance; and he taught for a time in the Christian school in Alexandria at the mouth of the Nile. He seems to have become a priest. He died in AD 214 or 215.

For some hundreds of years his name was included as one of the saints in the lists kept by the church in Rome, but because of some rather heretical ideas in his writings his name was dropped in 1586.

Origen

Another great Christian writer, Origen, about thirty years younger than Tertullian and Clement, lived in Alexandria. He too wrote in Greek. His father had been martyred in AD 202 while Origen was a teenager; and Origen never left the Church. He had a philosophical and enquiring mind. He seems to have written about a thousand books. He interpreted the books of the Old Testament to give everything in them a new and special meaning connected with Christ our Lord.

Saint Paul had sometimes used this kind of interpretation. Paul wrote, for example, in his letter to the Galatians, that the two sons of Abraham were prophetic foreshadowings or 'types' of things to come, Isaac of the Church, Ishmael of the non-Christians. Isaac, whose mother was a free woman and Abraham's proper wife, foreshadowed the Catholic Church. Ishmael, whose mother was a slave, could not inherit the promises made to Abraham for the Church, just as those outside cannot inherit the promises of Christ. Saint Irenaeus and other writers used similar ideas. Irenaeus saw in history, in our Lord's life and our redemption, a 'recapitulation' of what had gone before – a sort of pattern through which the Holy Spirit teaches us and shows us how everything we see and know is part of God's plan. Origen, writing in the same sort of way, developed all sorts of new ideas, mostly good, but some that we would find strange.

Demetrius, Bishop of Alexandria, made Origen head of the Christian school there; but he may not have been altogether happy with Origen's teaching. However, Origen succeeded in bringing a number of heretics, even including bishops, back into the Church. About AD 212 Origen visited Rome. For a time he thought of settling there. Julia Mamea, the mother of the emperor, had him visit her in Antioch. The bishops of Jerusalem and Caesarea made him very welcome in Palestine. They invited him to preach in their churches for three years. Bishop Demetrius of Alexandria disapproved of this. In AD 230 Origen was ordained priest in Palestine without getting permission from his own bishop in Egypt. Demetrius was very angry and called a meeting of bishops and priests at Alexandria to condemn Origen. He sent a report to Pope Pontianus who sided with him. But although Origen was prevented from living or working in the diocese of Alexandria he was not actually excommunicated. He went on preaching and writing.

When Decius became emperor in AD 249 a new persecution of Christians was started. Origen was imprisoned and cruelly tortured. We do not know exactly where he died; it must have been about AD 253, and he was buried in Tyre. Seventy years or so later, when the Christians were free to build public churches, the tomb of Origen could be seen in the cathedral there.

Some people, even in his lifetime, tried to use Origen's writings to back up wrong ideas. In one of his letters he complains that a heretic had changed what he wrote. According to the heretic, Origen had written that one day the devil will be saved; but Origen had not written this. However he did write that God the Son is not quite equal with God the

Father. He did think that we can be born again and again so that we can gradually become fit for heaven. And in addition to such mistaken or doubtful ideas the people who copied his books often made changes to fit their own ideas.

Rufinus of Aquilea, who lived in the next century, admired Origen's writings so much that he translated many of them into Latin. Because earlier copiers had made bad changes Rufinus tried to put these right by using what Origen wrote in one place in his books to correct what seemed wrong in another. By that time many heretics claimed to be following Origen's teaching. Saint Jerome, who had been a great friend of Rufinus, quarrelled with him bitterly about Origen. Some of Origen's own ideas, and many ideas of his more heretical followers were eventually condemned by the Church; but a number of his writings are still used. Some of them, and some of Tertullian's, are quoted in the decrees of the Second Vatican Council. Unlike Tertullian, Origen was a good and attractive man as well as a brilliant thinker.

Two very great saints, Saint Basil and Saint Gregory Nazianzus, in the fourth century made a collection of particularly useful writings of Origen. This collection they called *Philocalia*, which means love of Goodness.

7

Hippolytus

Saint Hippolytus (I)
Quarrel with the Popes

During his visit to Rome Origen had heard a sermon by a priest called Hippolytus. Hippolytus, like Tertullian and Origen, wrote many books. He wrote in Greek and he seems to have been taught at some time by Saint Irenaeus. He certainly studied the writings of the Greek philosophers and of the Gnostic heretics, so as to write more books showing where they were mistaken. Like Origen and Tertullian he seemed in his writings to say that God the Son is not quite equal to God the Father. Our Lord had said of himself, 'The Father is greater than I am', because he was living as a man for our sake – a man like ourselves with the body and mind of a man. In his human nature he obeyed the Father. But the Church came to realise that as the Son of God the Father he could also say truly, 'I and the Father are one'. Until this was spelled out more clearly at the Council of Nicea in AD 325 it was excusable if some good people made such mistakes.

Pope Callistus (AD 217 to 222) at one time had been tried by the Roman courts on a financial charge and had been condemned to hard labour in the mines in Sardinia. After his release from prison he was ordained a deacon. Pope Zephyrinus (199 to 217) put him in charge of a Christian cemetery which is still called the Catacomb of Saint Callistus. In AD 217 he was elected Pope.

The Roman laws had always forbidden marriage between slaves and free people. The Roman Emperors, Marcus and

Commodus, had insisted that such marriages were not only unlawful but also immoral. The children of such marriages were considered illegitimate. Pope Callistus, who had been a slave himself, decided that whatever Roman law said, among Christians a slave could marry a free person with the blessing of the Church.

Many bishops at that time were extremely strict, refusing to give absolution to those who committed very serious sins. When they did give absolution they insisted on long and hard public penances. Callistus was less strict. He gave absolution more readily to serious sinners as long as they did reasonably serious penance. He also ordained some married men as priests. Hippolytus disagreed with him over these things.

Some of the priests in Rome sided with Hippolytus. They said that a man like Callistus, who was so kind to sinners and slaves, could not himself be a good man and should not be Pope. Some bishops from outside Rome 'elected' Hippolytus, consecrated him, and said that he was the real bishop of Rome – the true Pope. Most Christians in Rome sided with Callistus. In one of his books Hippolytus wrote angrily that Callistus was kind to sinners just to make himself popular and to attract the Christian away from the stricter 'church' of Hippolytus. The things he wrote were so exaggerated that it is difficult to know what Callistus had really said or done. Hippolytus in any case wrote in another book that the consecration of a bishop certainly does give him the power to forgive sins, as our Lord had promised to the apostles.

Callistus was apparently martyred about the year AD 222. In the next year Urban was elected and consecrated Pope. He too was martyred eight years later and Pontianus became Pope. Hippolytus still continued as 'anti-Pope' until the new emperor, Maximus Thrax, exiled both Hippolytus and Pontianus to Sardinia. There at last Hippolytus was reconciled with the true Pope and gave up his claim. Pontianus too decided to resign so that the Romans could elect a new bishop to be Pope with no disagreement. Anteros, who was chosen, only lived for one year. Pontianus and Hippolytus both died in Sardinia during 236. The next Pope, Saint Fabian (236 to

255), had their bodies brought back to Rome and buried. A later Pope (Saint Damasus, 366 to 384) wrote that Hippolytus, before he died, had urged his followers to be reconciled to the true Popes and the Church. A statue of Hippolytus, made about the time of his death, is still kept in the Lateran Museum in Rome.

Saint Hippolytus (II)
'The Apostolic Tradition'

One of Hippolytus' books, *The Apostolic Tradition*, is very interesting. It describes the consecration of a bishop and the Mass to follow. The Eucharistic Prayer which Hippolytus gives is like the Eucharistic Prayer Number Two which we use today, though he adds: 'Let each bishop pray as he can. If he is able to pray with a grand and elevated prayer this is good. But if he prays and recites a prayer in a fixed form no one shall prevent him.'

Hippolytus also described the ceremony of Baptism. As the person to be baptised went down to the water the bishop or priest asked him questions: 'Do you believe in ...?', just as they do at baptism today. The questions followed what we now call the Apostles' Creed. The answer, 'I believe', was given after each section:– about God the Father, about Christ Jesus the Son of God, about the Holy Spirit in the Church and the resurrection of the dead. After each 'I believe' the priest laid his hand on the person's head and immersed him. The chief difference from today's ceremony was that each person to be baptised, unless he was sick or a young baby, used to go right down into the pool of water all three times. For babies and sick people water was simply poured on the head, and later – much later – this simpler way of baptism became generally used, as it is with us today. After baptism the priest, as he does now, anointed each new Christian with Holy Oil.

Hippolytus also gives prayers for Confirmation and a description of the ceremony. He calls it the 'sealing' of the Christian.

Novatian's Schism

After Pope Saint Fabian, who was martyred in AD 250, Cornelius was the next Bishop of Rome; and again there was trouble with an anti-Pope. Novatian had been ordained priest by Pope Fabian. He was a very intelligent writer, not as brilliant as Tertullian or Origen, but he wrote in good clear Latin. Some of his writings have helped the Church to find the best way of expressing what we believe about God the Father, God the Son and the Incarnation. But when Saint Fabian died Novatian wished to be chosen Pope to succeed him. For months it was difficult to choose and consecrate any new Pope. The Roman police made it difficult for Christians even to meet together; when they did meet, Novatian and his friends started arguments. In 256 the people and the nearby bishops chose Cornelius. Sixteen bishops joined together to consecrate him but Novatian objected. He demanded that any Christian who gave in to the persecution, who sacrificed to the Roman gods, or who merely pretended that he had sacrificed, to escape being tortured and killed, must never be forgiven – never allowed back into the Church whatever penance he did.

Novatian then hunted up three country bishops of places far away from Rome. When he got them to the city he shut them up with some of his own supporters. He seems even to have tried to make them drunk. Then, in the evening he persuaded or forced them to consecrate *him* 'Bishop of Rome'. In this way he and his friends started a new and 'schismatic' church which lasted for two or three hundred years. In the east of the empire they were called 'Katharoi' which means almost the same as 'Puritans'. Novatian, who started the schism, may have been killed in the persecution under the Emperor Valerian, before AD 260. He is often mentioned in the letters from Saint Cyprian, Bishop of Carthage, to Pope Cornelius.

8

Cyprian and the Popes

Saint Cyprian (I)
The Persecution of Decius

Cyprian was born about the year AD 200. He was brought up as a pagan and became, in time, an important lawyer in the city of Carthage, where he also taught public speaking. At some time he must have studied the Bible. When he was forty-six he was baptised a Christian. Only two years later, in the year 248, he was chosen to be bishop of Carthage, which was becoming the leading church for all the Roman territories of north Africa, from the western border of Egypt across to the Atlantic ocean – all the countries we now call Libya, Tunisia, Algeria and Morocco.

In the year after he was made bishop, the new emperor, Decius, decided that, to hold the empire together and to govern it he would have to make every Roman subject pay respect and make sacrifice to the old Roman gods. New orders were given to all the provinces and a general persecution was started, against the Christians and against anyone else who refused to sacrifice. Many Christians did refuse and were killed. Many more were put in prison. These were called 'confessors' because they 'confessed' that Jesus was the Lord and showed it by going to prison for his sake, even if they were not killed as martyrs. Some were brutally tortured. A few gave way under torture and sacrificed on the pagan altars. Some others bribed the Roman officials to give them certificates saying that they had sacrificed when in fact they had not. And large numbers obeyed the law, sacrificing as they were told to. Even among these there were many who truly believed in Christ and soon wished to come back into the Church to become proper Christians again.

It was clear that if Cyprian stayed in Carthage, where everyone knew him, he would quickly be arrested, tried and killed. At that time it would have been difficult to arrange a proper election of a new bishop to take charge of the diocese. They were having the same difficulty in Rome in the next year, AD 250. Part of the difficulty in Rome was caused by the ambition of Novatian to become bishop, and also by his harsh and unreasonable severity against Christians who lapsed. In Carthage they had similar difficulties with a deacon called Felicissimus who disliked Cyprian and who seems not to have been quite honest. In these circumstances Cyprian, with a few of his priests and deacons, went into hiding somewhere outside the city. From there he was able to help his people remarkably well through messengers and by letters.

He arranged for copies to be made of many of his letters so that the same information could be sent to several different churches in the African dioceses which came under the leadership of Carthage. He also kept in touch with the church in Rome. After he died, fifty-nine of his personal letters, with six more letters from councils of bishops of which he had been president, were collected into a book, along with sixteen letters which other people had sent to him. These sixteen were mostly from the bishops or clergy of Rome. Besides letters, Cyprian also wrote some short books.

Saint Cyprian (II)
Penance for the Lapsed

One of Cyprian's books was called *De Lapsis* – 'About the Lapsed'. He wrote very seriously about the sin of denying our Lord. He showed that getting certificates without actually making a sacrifice was still really a denial of our Lord. But he was very concerned to try to get the lapsed to confess their sin, to do penance and to come back into the Church.

He did not try to make reconciliation with the Church too easy. Our Lord had told the apostles, 'Those whose sins you forgive are forgiven. If you withhold forgiveness their sins are not forgiven.' Cyprian considered that rich Christians who had denied our Lord just to save their houses and money from confiscation should do penance for a long time – even years – to show that they were really sorry for deserting Christ so meanly. But he wished those who had been through torture and had only given in through weakness to be treated more kindly.

Some of the confessors in prison appealed to him for particular friends who had lapsed. They asked him to give these friends his 'peace', to lay his hands on them and admit them again to Holy Communion. Cyprian said that this would not be fair. He urged the lapsed to wait for a let-up in the persecution so that he could come back to Carthage and each case could be properly considered. The length of each one's penance should have some relation to his sin. In AD 250, while there was still no Pope in Rome, the priests and deacons there kept up a correspondence with Cyprian (letters number 8, 9, 20, 27, 30, 35, 36). They exchanged news about these questions; those in Rome were glad of Cyprian's encouragement and Cyprian was grateful for their advice.

This advice was about lapsed Christians who fell ill and were in danger of death. Cyprian agreed that, as in Rome, he should allow them to be given absolution and to receive Communion. Some who had lapsed once and then repented were arrested again and threatened with execution. They were likely to be braver the second time round. He gladly allowed them to be given the 'peace' of the Church and to receive our Lord's body and blood. He said they would need this strength to face martyrdom; and martyrdom, of course, would wipe away any stain of their first lapse.

Except for these special cases he made the lapsed wait till proper meetings could be held. He also did not like to ordain new priests while he was away from Carthage. In two of the letters to his own clergy and people he explains carefully why he had made exceptions to this rule. A young man called Aurelius had twice been imprisoned and both times had openly 'confessed', at the risk of his life, to being a Christian. Cyprian ordained him a 'reader' as a first step to making him a priest. Another confessor, Celerinus, had been in close confinement for nineteen days and had been tortured. His grandmother and two of his uncles had been martyred in Rome in an earlier persecution. When Cyprian had proposed to ordain him he had hesitated, but God had sent him a vision in the night telling him not to refuse. Cyprian wrote that he had ordained Celerinus too as a reader, and he hoped, when it became possible to hold a public ordination, to make both Aurelius and Celerinus priests with the approval of the other clergy and the people.

Saint Cyprian (III)
The Unity of the Church

Another book by Cyprian was called *De Ecclesiae Catholicae Unitate* – 'On the Unity of the Catholic Church'. It was written at the time when Novatian was setting himself up as a bishop against Cornelius, the true and obvious Bishop of Rome, and when in Carthage Felicissiumus was trying to oust Cyprian and set up another bishop in his place. Cyprian believed that all true bishops inherited Christian truth and Christ's authority directly from the apostles, with the guidance of the Holy Spirit. He wrote, 'The proof is simple and convincing ... The Lord says to Peter, "You are Peter (meaning Rock) and upon this rock I will build my Church, and the gates of hell shall not overcome it. I will give you the keys of the kingdom of heaven. What you bind on earth will be bound in heaven. What you loose on earth will be loosed in heaven."'

The next paragraph in Cyprian's book is important, but people understood it to mean more than he was prepared for. He seems to have re-written it later, leaving out the word 'primacy'. The first version seems to have been like this:-

> And the Lord says to him again after the resurrection, 'Feed my sheep.' It is on him that he builds the Church and to him that he trusts the sheep to feed. Although he gives the same power to all the apostles, yet he founded a single seat ["see" or bishopric]. He established by his authority the source and hallmark of oneness. Of course the others were all that Peter

was, but Peter was given the primacy. It is made clear that there is only one Church and one seat. So even if all are shepherds we are shown only one flock. The flock is to be fed by all the apostles in agreement together. If anyone does not hold on to this oneness of Peter, does he imagine that he still holds the faith? If he leaves the seat of Peter on whom the Church is built, is he still sure that he is in the Church? The authority of the bishops forms a unity. Each holds his part in the whole.

In AD 251, writing from his hiding place to all his people, Cyprian said, 'God is one, and Christ one, and the Church one, and the seat established on Peter by the voice of the Lord, one'. Later on in the same year 251 Cornelius was elected and consecrated Pope. The collection of Cyprian's letters includes nine letters to Cornelius and two from Cornelius to Cyprian. At this time the followers of Novatian and Felicissimus were travelling between Rome, Carthage and other cities, trying to divide the churches from one another in the hope that somewhere the Novatianists would be accepted. Some of these men had gone to Rome to make all sorts of accusations against Cyprian. Cornelius was evidently worried and wrote to Cyprian a letter which has been lost. Cyprian's long reply shows that he was upset; he could not bear the idea that Cornelius should believe the slanders of bad men about him. 'They dare to sail [to Rome] and bring letters from heretics and blasphemers to the seat of Peter, to the principal church, the church from which the unity of the bishops springs.' He thought even that Cornelius was frightened of them.

Saint Cyprian (IV)
Rome, Africa, Spain, France

In 251 the persecution in Africa stopped for a time and Cyprian was able to hold a council in Carthage to settle many things which had had to wait while he was in hiding. He held more councils of this kind, one every year, until the persecution began again under the Emperor Valerian. After the council of 252 he and the forty-three African bishops wrote a report to Cornelius in Rome.

On 14th September 252 Cornelius was martyred by the Roman authorities. During the following year Lucius became Pope. Cyprian and his priests wrote a letter of congratulation to the new Bishop of Rome. Lucius had already spent some time in prison, so Cyprian congratulated him even more on the 'honour' of his confession of Christ the Lord.

In the same year, 253, a gang of barbarians invaded Numidia, the province which is now part of Algeria. They captured a group of Christians including eight local bishops. Cyprian quickly collected a large sum of money to send to them, along with a most kind and sympathetic letter. That year he was able to hold a council of sixty-six bishops and senior clergy, at which he was able to correct some things that were going wrong: in some places priests had been celebrating Mass without wine; in other places the bishops had been refusing to baptise babies until they were eight days old.

By this time Cyprian was becoming so well known that bishops from as far away as Spain wrote to ask him for help. Two of the Spanish bishops, Martial of Merida and Basilides, had sacrificed to the gods and had lived like pagans during the persecution of Decius. The other Christians forced them to resign. New bishops, Sabinus and Felix, were elected and consecrated. Basilides and Martial went to Rome to try to get the Pope to make the Spanish Christians give them back their sees. It is plain, from Cyprian's reply to a letter from Felix, that Basilides had been lying and trying to deceive the Pope. Another Spanish bishop (also called Felix) wrote from Zaragoza to Cyprian confirming what had been written from Merida about Basilides. 'Our colleague, Stephen [the new Pope],' wrote Cyprian in his reply, 'is far away and does not know the truth of what has happened'. Cyprian supported the new bishops.

Another bishop, Faustinus, of Lyons in France, wrote both to Cyprian and to Pope Stephen about Marcian, bishop of Arles, who had joined the followers of Novatian and was insisting that none of those who had lapsed, however sorry they were for their sin and whatever penance they were ready to do, could ever be received back into the Church or be allowed Holy Communion. Cyprian wrote to Rome urging Pope Stephen to send an official letter to all the dioceses in

France, warning them against Marcian and excommunicating him. 'There could not be different opinions among us in whom there is one spirit,' he wrote. 'Let us know plainly who has been made bishop in Arles in place of Marcian, so that we may know whom we should send people to, and whom we should write to.'

Saint Cyprian (V)
Baptism by Heretics

Cyprian was mistaken in thinking that 'there *could not* be different opinions' between bishops. By the year AD 255 he discovered that he and his colleague and brother, Stephen, had different opinions about baptising people who had been baptised by Novatian. He wrote about this, quite angrily at times, to several priests and bishops. After the council at Carthage in 255, he and thirty other bishops wrote to the bishops of Numidia giving all the reasons why the church in Carthage believed that baptism by a heretic was no baptism at all. The problem had been discussed forty years earlier at a previous council in Carthage. From that time any heretics – anyone in north or north-west Africa who had been baptised by heretics – if they wished to become Catholics had had to be 'baptised' again. In Rome, and in western Europe and Egypt, when Christians had been properly baptised as our Lord commanded, even if the person baptising them was a heretic outside the Church, the bishops would not baptise them a second time when they became Catholics. It is the sacrament which brings God's grace, even if the person who pours the water is a heretic or a sinner.

Pope Stephen's letters about baptism have been lost, but Cyprian, in the course of a letter to another African bishop called Pompey, gives a quotation from one of Stephen's replies in these words: 'If anyone comes to you from any heresy whatever ... hands should be laid on them in penance. The heretics themselves do not baptise those who come to them from other heresies but only receive them in Communion.'

If Cyprian has quoted exactly what Stephen wrote, then

Stephen's letter was carelessly written. Some heretics baptise without using our Lord's words, and that is not true baptism. Besides, what heretics do about one another does not seem really a good argument for what Catholics ought to do about heretics. But Stephen, as Pope, as Bishop of Rome, as successor of Saint Peter, was giving the true Catholic teaching on this, even if his letter was hurriedly written. Saint Cyprian was mistaken.

The argument was not settled at that time. Fifty-eight years later, in AD 314, at a council at Arles in France, Catholic bishops generally recognised that Pope Stephen had been right. The African bishops, at another council in 346, changed over to the Roman practice. And sometime during the debate Cyprian seems to have rewritten the paragraph about Saint Peter in his book *On the Unity of the Catholic Church*.

Saint Cyprian (VI)
The Unity of the Bishops

The second version of the paragraph is longer and uses many of the sentences used in the first. It does not mention the 'primacy' given to Peter. Cyprian still writes, 'no doubt the other apostles as well were all that Peter was'. He adds:-

> 'This oneness [of the Church] we must hold on to firmly – especially we who are bishops, who have authority in the Church – so as to show that the bishops' power is one and undivided too.'

As in the first version he goes on to write, 'The authority of the bishops forms a unity of which each holds his part'.

He believed that the Holy Spirit guided all the bishops to keep them united. This was partly true, especially in the first centuries when it was more difficult for the bishops to keep in touch with one another. But he hardly faced up to the fact that even good bishops sometimes get hold of mistaken ideas and need to check these with the teaching of the Bishops of Rome. Our Lord's promises to Saint Peter did give to his successors a primacy. Saint Cyprian's actions – his efforts always to ensure agreement between Rome and Carthage – showed the way in which the Holy Spirit was leading the Church. Nevertheless he was slow to recognise that the bishops of Carthage had been wrong on this point for forty years.

Saint Cyprian (VII)
The Persecution of Valerian

The last letter about baptism in the collection of Saint Cyprian's letters was one written to Cyprian by a bishop called Firmilian of Caesarea in Cappadocia, now part of Turkey. It agrees with Cyprian's arguments, but it criticises Stephen so harshly that some people think it may have put Cyprian off and made him unwilling to go on arguing. In any case Pope Saint Stephen was martyred in 257. Valerian had become emperor in 253 and around 256 he started a new, severe persecution of Christians.

The last six letters in the collection are all about the new persecution. Nine African bishops in three different places were arrested with their priests, deacons and other Christians. Cyprian wrote a letter to them all and separate copies must have been made for each group. In the letter he says he is proud of them. He addresses them as though they were already martyrs. He is sympathetic, affectionate and encouraging, looking forward to their happiness when, with Christ, they have won their victory and come to heaven. Each of the three groups sent back letters of gratitude for his encouragement and good example. In August of 257 Cyprian himself was arrested and exiled to a place called Curubis. He stayed there in a country place belonging to the church. During this exile he could not send letters because the priests and deacons who used to take his letters for him were all prevented by the police from travelling anywhere. Eventually he succeeded in sending someone to Rome who managed to report back on what was happening in the capital.

The only letter which Cyprian wrote from Curubis was to Bishop Successus. He gave news of what he had been able to learn about a new instruction which the emperor had sent to the Roman Senate. The emperor had ordered that Christian bishops, priests and deacons should be punished at once. Members of the Senate, knights and other important Romans who had become Christians would lose their rank, and all their goods would be confiscated. If they still continued to be Christians they were to be beheaded. Married women were to be sent into exile. Any of those who were working for Caesar's household who would not give up Christianity were to be made slaves.

Cyprian had also heard that Pope Sixtus II had been executed on 6th August 258, a year after the martyrdom of Pope Stephen. Four deacons had been executed with the Pope.

Saint Cyprian (VIII)
Martyrdom

Cyprian's last letter was written from a place where he was hiding on the advice of his friends. Police had been sent to Curubis to take him to Utica for trial because the Roman pro-consul, Galerius Maximus, was not in Carthage at the time. He wrote to his priests, deacons and to all the people of his diocese to let them know that he agreed to stay in hiding until the pro-consul returned to Carthage. He wished to be tried in that city, to speak more openly to the people and to be executed in Carthage itself, the place where he was bishop, so as to be an honour and an example to his own people.

He asked all the Christians meanwhile to keep quiet and be tranquil. 'Do not stir up any sort of disturbance,' he wrote. 'None of the Christians should offer himself to the pagans to be a martyr. The one whom the police arrest and who is put on trial is the one who ought to speak out. God will speak through him at that time.' The other Christians should be witnesses for Cyprian. He was arrested on 13th September 258, tried, and beheaded the next day.

In the same year, 258, eight Christians including some of Cyprian's clergy were imprisoned on a false charge. A priest called Victor was executed immediately. The others were kept in prison and half-starved for several months. Some

Cyprian and the Popes

quarrels broke out among them; but one of them called Montanus had a dream which seemed to be sent by God, showing that they especially should be kind and charitable with one another.

Eventually they were tried. The judge sentenced the clergy, deacons and readers, to be executed. One of them called Lucius was so ill that he set out early for the place of execution to make sure he did not get left behind. Another, called Flavian, was reprieved because even the pagans liked him and said in evidence that he was not a deacon. He insisted that he was, and eventually he convinced the judge of this. He was beheaded three days later.

In the same year in Cirta (now called Constantine, in Algeria) more Christians were arrested, tortured and killed in a mass execution. The condemned men were lined up in rows and the executioner cut off head after head. Their martyrdom was described afterwards by a man who had been imprisoned with them but who was afterwards released.

In AD 260, the Emperor Valerian was defeated, captured and killed by the Persians. He had made his son Gallienus joint emperor with him to share his work by being responsible for the western half of the empire. Gallienus had not enforced the law against the Christians in France or Britain. When he found himself sole emperor he made an edict stopping the persecution throughout the empire, and giving back to the Christians some of the property which had been confiscated. From this time until 297 there was very little persecution in any part of the empire. Many new Christians were baptised. Proper churches were openly built where Christians could gather together in large numbers, as they do today.

9

Dionysius of Alexandria
Gregory Thaumaturgus
Felix of Nola

Martyrologies

When people of our own town die in war we like to think that they died bravely for us and for our country. Often we put their names on war memorials. During the Roman persecutions the Christians, with more reason, began to make lists of martyrs (Martyrologies) preserving the names of those who died bravely for our faith and for love of our Lord. Jesus had said, 'No one has greater love than this, to give up his life for his friends. I have called you friends.' But martyrdom is only a sort of proof of their love and courage. The Greek word 'martur' means 'witness'. It is possible to be a martyr without being a saint – without a true love of our Lord. It is also possible to be a saint – a hero – brave, just, temperate, wise, with faith and trust in our Lord, loving God and our fellow men generously and wholeheartedly – without getting killed for it.

Between the time of Nero (say AD 64) and that of Constantine (AD 313) so many of the most notable Christians were martyred that it became common to expect that a really good Christian should be martyred; and among Christians they were accustomed to talk about martyrs more than about other kinds of saints. But there were some saints – Saint

John, Saint Irenaeus – who were honoured by the Christians even though they were not, so far as we know, actually killed for their faith.

During the years 260 to 297, between the persecutions under Valerian and those under Diocletian, there were hardly any martyrdoms or imprisonments of confessors; so the Christians began to pay more attention to other good and holy people. They honoured them along with the martyrs and confessors, and included their names in the martyrologies.

Saint Apollonia

Around this time the great Greek city of Alexandria in Egypt became very unruly. In AD 249, even before the persecution ordered by the Emperor Decius, there was a serious anti-Christian riot during which several Christians were killed. The most important was a deaconess called Apollonia. The rioters hit her in the face, knocking out her teeth. They made a big fire in the street and said that if she did not give up her religion they would throw her in. For answer she walked into the fire by herself and was burned to death.

Saint Dionysius of Alexandria

Apollonia's bishop, Dionysius, had at one time studied under Origen, and later was put in charge of the catechetical school, that is the school for teaching the Christian faith, which Origen had made famous. In 247 he was made bishop. At the beginning of the persecution under Decius he was arrested but he was able to escape. Like Cyprian he went into hiding, yet managed to look after his diocese through letters and messengers. In the lull between Decius and Valerian, 251 to 253, he returned to the city. During the discussions about those who had lapsed under the persecution and who afterwards wished to come back to the Church, he was one of the more lenient bishops. In 257, in Valerian's persecution, he was again arrested and was expelled from Alexandria. He returned in 261 and went on with his work in the diocese, with his studies and with his writings. He died in AD 265 – an important saint, not a martyr.

The Martyrs of the Plague

Among the writings of Dionysius of Alexandria is the letter from which we know about the martyrdom of Saint Apollonia. But rioting and murders were not the only troubles in that city during his life. In 262 there was a terrible epidemic of plague. Most of the Christians in the city behaved wonderfully. They cared for the sick and the dying, helping them, bringing them food and medicine when they could, comforting them, nursing them, often catching the disease from them and dying with them. 'This Christian generosity', wrote Dionysius, 'seemed little short of martyrdom itself'. Ever since that time the Christians who died there have been called 'The Martyrs of the Plague at Alexandria'.

Saint Gregory Thaumaturgus

Another saint of this time who was not martyred became extremely popular in the Greek-speaking world. This was Gregory of Neocaesarea in Pontus. The town is 200 miles east of Ankara and is now called Niksar. This Gregory was born around AD 213. As a young man he travelled with his brother through Egypt, Greece, Lebanon and Palestine. He was in Caesarea when Origen was teaching there and seems to have studied for five years with Origen. Eventually he became a Christian and was persuaded to become a priest. On his return to Pontus a bishop of a neighbouring town got him to accept consecration as bishop of his own city although he was still young – not yet thirty. The rest of his life was spent making the city Christian. He died early in the 270s.

Most of what we know about Gregory Thaumaturgus, which means 'wonder worker', was written more than a hundred years later by another Saint Gregory – Gregory of Nyssa. Some information comes also from the writings of

Saint Basil the Great. Basil and Gregory of Nyssa were brothers. Their father, also called Basil, had been a well-known teacher of public speaking in Neocaesarea. Altogether four of the children of the older Basil became saints. His eldest child was called Macrina (Macrina the Younger) after her grandmother. Besides Macrina, Basil and Gregory, another son, Peter of Sebastea, is also reckoned a saint.

The grandmother, Macrina the Elder, is the link with Gregory Thaumaturgus. It was from him, according to Basil the Great, that his grandmother had learned her holiness. 'She stored up his words which had been memorised and handed down to her.' Through her, her son and all her grandchildren learned much about the older Gregory. It is not certain whether she actually met him. More probably she was born soon after he died. In any case, through her he had great influence on the remarkable family of Basil.

According to Gregory of Nyssa there were only seventeen Christians in Neocaesarea when the Thaumaturgus became bishop; and when he died there were only seventeen people in the city who were *not* Christian. The younger Gregory also tells of very many miracles which God worked through the older Gregory. Some of these stories are so extraordinary that it seems likely they grew and became exaggerated during the hundred years before they were written down. There is however good evidence that, with God working through him, he lived up to his name of 'miracle worker.' He is the earliest saint who is recorded to have seen a vision of our Lady and Saint John.

Saint Felix of Nola

Another saint of this time, whose miracles may have been exaggerated over the years before they were put down in writing, was Felix of Nola, a town near Naples. His tomb became a place of pilgrimage after his death.

Paulinus, who was born at Bordeaux in AD 353, was attracted by the reputation of Felix. He was so attracted that in 395 he went with his wife to live in Nola. In 409 he was chosen bishop of the town. He built a large new church in honour of Felix and wrote many poems for his feast-day. From these poems we know something of the life of Felix. He was ordained priest, and in AD 250, during the persecution of Decius, he was arrested, imprisoned and very harshly treated. His bishop, Maximus, had gone into hiding all alone. Felix, while in prison, saw a vision of an angel who told him that Maximus needed his help. With the assistance of the angel Felix escaped and went in search of Maximus. He found him cold, hungry and unconscious; but he was able to revive him. However the bishop was so weak that Felix had to carry him home by night.

When the emperor died, Felix came out of hiding to go on with his work as a priest, but the pagans tried to lock him up again and he was forced to go back into hiding for another six months. A well-known story about him says that while he was concealed in a ruined building a spider quickly spun a web over the entrance. When the police saw the spider's web they thought that Felix could not have gone inside and they failed to find him. After Bishop Maximus died the Christians wanted Felix to be the next bishop but he insisted that Quintus was senior to him and refused. Quintus had been ordained priest just five days earlier than Felix, so Quintus was made bishop and he and Felix worked closely together.

In 260 when the Emperor Gallienus ordered that Christians should get back the property which had been confiscated from them during the persecution, Felix was urged to make a claim for his land, but he refused. He said that as a poor man without earthly possessions he was more sure of possessing Christ. Instead he rented a small farm, less than three acres, where he managed to grow enough food to keep alive and to have a little over to give to the very poor. He died not long afterwards.

Although Saint Paulinus lived about a hundred and fifty years later he believed that all the graces he received were through the prayers of Saint Felix. He himself saw miracles worked at Felix's tomb and he heard of many more which had happened over the years.

10

The Great Persecution

Years of Peace

During the forty years, AD 260 to 300, the Church grew in numbers and the Christians became much more important in the community. They built places for worship. They made copies of the scriptures, the New Testament as well as the Old. Some Christians, and even some bishops, were given government appointments by the Roman authorities or their allies.

Paul of Samosata was a very rich man who was able to get the support of several local bishops. He became bishop of Antioch, the chief church in Syria, and in 260 he was appointed a procurator under Zenobia, queen of Palmyra (to the north of Damascus). He began a new heresy saying that our Lord did not come 'from above' but 'from below'. This alarmed Saint Dionysius of Alexandria and other bishops, who arranged a synod to find out what his teaching meant. At the first meeting Paul succeeded in pretending to be a good Catholic, but by 265 when they held a further synod, it was clear that he did not believe that our Lord was the Son of God. In fact he was making a new religion with himself as the centre. In a third synod in 266 he was excommunicated. A new bishop of Antioch called Domnus was appointed in 269, but Paul was able to stay in the city under the protection of Zenobia. In 272 the Emperor Aurelian made war on Zenobia, defeated her and captured Antioch. After this the Catholics appealed to the emperor to help them in their dispute. Although the emperor was a pagan he decided that

120 *Apostles and Martyrs*

Domnus was entitled to the bishopric. He may have been influenced by knowing that Domnus was supported by the bishops of Italy and the church of Rome. Paul of Samosata then had to leave Antioch in disgrace.

The Great Persecution (I)
Diocletian

This same period of forty years which was peaceful for the Christian Church was a time of great trouble for the Roman Empire. In 270, when Aurelian became emperor, German tribes were attacking the northern frontiers. Gaul (France) set up an independent empire. The Persians, ten years earlier, had defeated, captured and killed the Emperor Valerian. Zenobia was building up an independent kingdom including Syria and Egypt where much of the food for the city of Rome and other parts of Italy was grown. There were epidemics of plague in several parts of the empire. There were riots, almost amounting to civil war, in Rome and other cities. Aurelian managed to reunite the empire and restore some sort of order. The Romans gave him the title of *Restitutor Orbis* – 'Restorer of the World'. They worshipped him as a god in his own lifetime; but after only ruling for five years he was assassinated.

The pagans began to feel that the confusion and disorder were so bad that only the gods – the old Roman gods who, according to their legends, had made Rome great – could restore their empire – their world – to peace and civilisation. Each new emperor they hoped would be the one whom the gods would help to set the world right again. After the death of Aurelian the next emperor, Probus, governed well from 276 to 282, but his fellow-soldiers disliked his strict discipline and killed him. Diocletian became emperor in 284 and seemed at first to be having more success.

Diocletian soon decided that the empire was too wide and the problems were too many for one man. In 286 he chose a second emperor, Maximian, to control and defend the west. In 293 he chose two more rulers to work under Maximian and himself and to succeed them eventually as emperors.

Constantius Chlorus shared Maximian's responsibilities in the west; Galerius shared Diocletian's in the east. They were each given the title of Caesar. The two senior emperors kept the title of Augustus.

Diocletian also decided that the only way to bind the Romans together was through the old Roman religion. He claimed that he was led by the spirit of Jupiter, and Maximian by the spirit of Hercules. He made himself distant and unapproachable. He changed the role of the emperor from that of a leading citizen, a military commander, into that of a mysterious and absolute ruler – a god.

Already in 295 Diocletian was pictured as a god on metal tags used in the army, and a Christian soldier in Numidia was martyred for refusing to accept such a tag. In 298 a Christian captain, a centurion called Marcellus, refused to take an oath to the emperor-god. He threw down his sword, and was executed for doing so. In different parts of the empire other soldiers resigned or were dismissed, and some were killed for refusing to accept that the emperors were gods. In AD 303 and 304 Diocletian and the other three emperors issued four edicts which started the last and worst of the Roman persecutions of the Church.

The first of these edicts ordered all church buildings to be demolished so that Christians should have no place to meet. It ordered all Christian books to be destroyed. It ordered various kinds of degradation for Christian people so that they should lose any position of authority in society.

The second edict ordered all priests and officers of the church to be imprisoned. The third edict ordered that all those in prison who sacrificed to the gods should be set free. It also ordered that every means should be used to make the prisoners sacrifice. The fourth edict ordered that Christians who refused to sacrifice should be killed.

Although all four emperors had their names on these edicts it seems that Constantius did no more than order the church buildings to be destroyed. From the beginning of this persecution it was in the eastern half of the empire that the Christians suffered most, under Diocletian, and especially under Galerius. In the lands under Maximian – Spain, north Africa and Italy – there were also many martyrs. Pope Saint

Marcellinus was killed in 304 and it was not until the year 307 that the Romans were able to choose and consecrate their next bishop.

Eusebius (I)
Saint Pamphilus

Two writers have given us some account of the terrible treatment of the Christians in these years. One account is in a book called *On the Deaths of Persecutors* by Lactantius. Lactantius was born in Africa about AD 240 or a little later. He wrote in Latin and was given, by Diocletian, a position as teacher in Nicomedia, Diocletian's capital city (now Izmit, in Turkey, fifty miles east of Istanbul). When the persecution began Lactantius went to Italy and then to France. He died about AD 320 at Trier in the Rhineland.

The other writer, Eusebius of Caesarea in Palestine, was about thirty-nine when the four edicts were issued. By then he was a priest, working with his friend Pamphilus. Both Pamphilus and Eusebius worked together to collect books by earlier Christian writers and records of the various churches. They formed one of the most important Christian libraries, and both men, in turn, wrote books. Pamphilus was the hero of Eusebius' life. He was imprisoned in 307 and Eusebius visited him in prison. He died a martyr in AD 309 or 310 and Eusebius wrote a special book in his honour. He also took his name as a sort of second Christian name – 'Eusebius Pamphili'.

Eusebius is best known as the author of the first history of the Christian Church. He wrote this in ten books and today it is usually printed in two volumes. The later books in this history describe some of the horrible tortures which Eusebius himself saw being used in Palestine, in Egypt and in Lebanon during the persecutions. This history also gives very many quotations, word for word, from earlier writers, often from books and letters which have now been lost. Without Eusebius we should know much less about the story of the early Church.

The Great Persecution (II)
Nine Emperors

In 305 Diocletian and Maximian both retired. The two Caesars, Galerius and Constantius, were each given the title of Augustus. Maximin Daia and Severus were made Caesars. The following year Constantius died and his soldiers proclaimed his son Augustus. This son was Constantine. Galerius agreed unwillingly to accept Constantine as joint ruler. In Rome a son of Maximian, called Maxentius, set himself up as Augustus and made himself ruler over most of Italy. In 307 Severus died but Maximian came out of retirement and had himself declared Augustus again. Before the end of 307 Galerius had his friend Licinius also declared Augustus.

Among these nine different emperors Galerius seems to have been the most violent persecutor of the Christians. His hatred of Christianity may have influenced Diocletian, the senior emperor, in drawing up the edicts of 303 and 304. Maximian, Maximian's son Maxentius, and Maximin Daia, all carried on the persecution in different parts of the empire, although Christians were not the only victims of the atrocities committed by these men. Maxentius especially seems to have taken a personal delight in brutality.

Wars naturally broke out between some of these rival rulers. Severus had been made Caesar at Galerius' demand before Diocletian had retired. He became Augustus in 306 and in 307 Galerius sent him to attack Maxentius in Rome but he was defeated and fled to Ravenna. There he was captured, brought back to Rome and killed.

Maximian, almost as soon as Maxentius had declared him Augustus for the second time, turned against him although he was his son. He went east to try to get help from his former colleagues, Diocletian and Galerius. Then he tried to trap Constantine, but in the end Constantine killed him in 310.

In that year Galerius developed cancer with all sorts of revolting complications. People said it was God's punishment for his terrible treatment of the Christians; and at last in April of 311 he issued an Edict of Toleration of Christianity. In the edict he said he would issue detailed orders for freeing those in prison and restoring churches and property; but he died in May – a horrible death.

In 312 Constantine in his turn moved against Maxentius. He advanced to the walls of Rome. Before the battle he dreamed that he should paint crosses on the shields of his army. Next day he defeated the army of Maxentius at the Milvian Bridge and Maxentius was drowned in the river Tiber. The story is told that during the night before the battle Constantine saw a cross in the sky with the words *In hoc signo vinces*: 'In this sign you will conquer'. Certainly after this time Constantine's military standard depicted a spearhead forming the cross with the first two letters of Christ in Greek, XP, enclosed in a circle.

Maximin Daia pretended to accept Galerius' edict of toleration of the Christians, but when some of the more pagan places asked his permission to expel Christians from their cities he encouraged them. He appointed new head priests in these cities and allowed them to maltreat, torture and kill Christians under pretence of keeping order. After the death of Maxentius, Maximin Daia set out with an army to fight Licinius, but Licinius, with a much smaller army, was able to defeat him at Heraclea Pontica (now Eregli) on the sea coast a hundred miles east of Istanbul, on 30th April 313. Maximin escaped back to Nicomedia, and from there he fled to Tarsus where he died in August.

Constantine and Christianity

Diocletian, after his abdication, took little part in the struggles of the rival emperors. He too died in 313. It was at Milan in February that year that Constantine finally decided, with the agreement of Licinius, to recognise Christianity as a legitimate religion. On 13th June Licinius published a rescript or order for the eastern half of the empire which practically marked the end of the last and worst of the Roman persecutions.

Licinius had come to Milan in 313 to marry Constantine's sister, yet soon afterwards he turned against him. His efforts in 314 to overthrow Constantine were unsuccessful. Some years later, in 321, he prepared a more serious war. By this time Constantine, although he was still not baptised, was generally considered to be a Christian emperor, so Licinius expelled all the Christians in his own court in the east. He forced all the government officials and army officers in his half of the empire to sacrifice to the pagan gods. He forbad synods or large assemblies of Christians. Although his laws were much less severe than those of twenty years earlier, many of the local governors began torturing and executing Christians again. Then in 324 Constantine defeated him. He was executed. Constantine became ruler of the whole empire, in which Christianity was now the principal religion.

At the height of the persecution Christians had other things to think about than keeping records. Many outstandingly courageous martyrs became well known by name and some of their names have become popular through the Christian world, although the only written accounts we have of them were written so much later that we cannot now distinguish between what is true and what is legend in their stories. In most of these cases there is no reason to doubt that they were indeed heroic saints to whom we may pray, but it is difficult to write about them in a book which tries to include only what is genuinely historical.

11

The Arian Heresy

Saint Lucian and Arius

One of the martyrs in the last years of persecution under Maximin Daia had been Lucian of Antioch. He had been a priest of that church and head of the school of Christian teaching. This school at Antioch had developed a tradition of interpreting scripture as literally as possible, while the school at Alexandria, from the time of Origen, had shown more interest in allegorical interpretation. Lucian was a well known scholar who carefully corrected the Greek translation of the Old Testament. He also revised the Greek of the four Gospels. In doing this he took some of our Lord's sayings ('The Father is greater than I', or 'Times ... known only to the Father') to show that our Lord was not quite equal to the Father – that he was not quite God. Because of this Lucian was excommunicated in 269, but about fifteen years later he and the school at Antioch came to realise that they had been too literal. They had not paid proper attention to the saying of our Lord, 'I and the Father are one,' and the accusation from the Jews that 'He made himself equal to God.' They submitted to the bishops and came back to the true Christian and Catholic belief.

Unfortunately a priest of Alexandria called Arius had taken up the wrong ideas of Lucian and began to spread them. Lucian meanwhile was imprisoned at the beginning of Diocletian's persecution and remained in prison for more than eight years. He was twice brought out for trial. Each time he defended himself well and refused to renounce Christ.

Finally, in 312, he was martyred at Nicomedia. Both the true, 'orthodox' Christians and the followers of Arius – the Arians – recognised him as a hero and a saint.

Eusebius (II)
The Council of Nicea

The wrong ideas of Arius troubled the whole Church, and especially the Christians in the eastern half of the empire, for many years. Arius' own bishop, Alexander, excommunicated him at a council of bishops in Alexandria and Arius wrote to a number of different bishops complaining that this was unfair. The historian, Eusebius, had now become bishop of Caesarea and was sorry for him. Another Eusebius, bishop of Nicomedia, the eastern capital, and some other eastern bishops supported Arius much more strongly. Eusebius of Caesarea was not an 'Arian'. He wished to follow whatever the Church as a whole agreed on, provided only that it agreed with holy scripture.

The Church became so disturbed that the Emperor Constantine decided to get the dispute settled. He arranged a great council of bishops, including representatives from the Pope, the bishop of Rome, who met at Nicea (Iznik) thirty or forty miles south-west of Nicomedia, in AD 325. This was the first General Council of the whole Church. Constantine himself attended and had Eusebius of Caesarea to sit next to him on his right. Eusebius made the opening speech. Constantine made a short reply in Latin.

The main business of the Council was the discussion of the Church's teaching about our Lord. Eusebius took the lead by giving to the Council the words of the Creed used at baptisms in his own church in Caesarea. It was the creed which he had accepted at his own baptism and which he had repeated when he was ordained priest. After discussion the Council accepted this creed with the addition of the word 'homoousion' – 'one substance'. The bishops made some other additions, but this word was the really important one. They finally accepted the 'Credo' – the 'I believe' – more or less as we use it today at Sunday Mass. It includes the words 'Jesus Christ ... *one in substance* [or *of one being*] with the Father.'

The Council went on to condemn several of the ideas being spread by Arius. As these condemned ideas did not come from the Bible Eusebius agreed with the Council's condemnation.

Eusebius (III)
Sabellianism

An opposite sort of heresy, saying that God the Father and God the Son were only one Person, had been started a hundred years earlier by a Roman Priest called Sabellius. He had been excommunicated in AD 217 by Pope Callistus. Eusebius of Caesarea became involved in an argument with Eustathius, Bishop of Antioch, who seemed to be a follower of Sabellius. Eustathius was deposed by a synod at Antioch in 330. Most of the bishops who attended this synod were more or less Arians. When they offered the bishopric of Antioch to Eusebius it seemed that they were claiming him as one of the Arian party. But he refused the offer.

Saint Athanasius and the Arians

In the years 334 and 335 Eusebius of Caesarea was indirectly involved in the struggle between Athanasius and the other Eusebius – the Arian Eusebius of Nicomedia. Saint Athanasius had been at the Council of Nicea while he was still a deacon, helping his bishop, Alexander. Alexander died in 328 and Athanasius was chosen the next bishop of Alexandria. He continued as bishop for forty-six years, but seventeen of those years he spent in exile. He was the first of the four teachers or 'Fathers' of the Greek-speaking church who are usually called 'the Great' (Athanasius the Great, Basil the Great, etc.).

The Arians, after they were condemned at Nicea in 325, soon came to see Athanasius as their chief enemy. They tried to get the emperor to call another council at Caesarea where they hoped to get a majority of friendly or neutral bishops to depose Athanasius. Athanasius refused to attend. In 335 Constantine ordered him to come to a new meeting in Tyre.

Athanasius went, but the Arians there behaved so badly that Athanasius slipped away secretly. The emperor had not been present at the meeting in Tyre so Athanasius sailed to Constantinople (Istanbul) to speak to Constantine personally.

Constantine at this time had decided to celebrate his thirty years as Augustus with the dedication of the great new church he had been building in Jerusalem – the first Church of the Holy Sepulchre.

Arius meanwhile wrote a letter to the emperor in which he seemed to accept the decisions of Nicea. As a result, at the celebrations in Jerusalem Arius and his friends were allowed back into the Church. Athanasius however was able to convince the emperor that the meeting in Tyre had been unfair; so Constantine ordered the bishops concerned to meet again in Constantinople. The Arians obeyed but the others did not. Arius himself died at this time, but his friends managed to get Constantine to have Athanasius expelled from Egypt. The emperor was less interested in the rights and wrongs of heresy than in having peace in the important church of Alexandria.

Eusebius (IV)
In Praise of Constantine

Eusebius of Caesarea had accepted the condemnation of Arius at Nicea though he does not seem to have been very strongly opposed to the Arians. He showed himself far more resolute against the opposite heresy and, at the synod in Constantinople, he took the lead in the condemnation of Bishop Marcellus of Ancyra who was a Sabellian.

As the struggle against the Arian heresy was a main concern of the Church in these years, and as Saint Athanasius was eventually recognised as the hero of this struggle, Eusebius appeared to many people to be too neutral – worried only about Sabellianism, the opposite heresy. In later years some writers condemned him as pro-Arian. Others however – both in the east and in the west – thought he was a saint. Athanasius himself seems never to have regarded him as an enemy or as a heretic.

Before the end of Constantine's 'Thirty Year' celebrations Eusebius again had an opportunity to make an important speech in the new capital.

This was his speech 'In Praise of the Emperor'. Constantine clearly liked him.

Constantine died on 22nd May 337, two years after Eusebius' speech. Eusebius himself died two or three years later. He was an important writer and a good bishop. He may have been over-enthusiastic in his praise of Constantine. His attitude to the Arians may have been less straightforward than Athanasius' friends would have liked. But he was no heretic; and certainly his 'History' has been of great value to the Church.

12

Antony

Saint Antony (I)
Family

Saint Antony, perhaps in contrast to Eusebius of Caesarea, was certainly a Christian hero. He lived through the years of peace between Valerian and Diocletian, through the years of the great persecution, and for another forty years into the new age of the Christian emperors. When he died Saint Athanasius, who knew him personally, wrote his life – the first Christian biography of a saint.

Antony was born in AD 251 in a well-to-do Egyptian Christian family. While his parents were alive he lived with them. He preferred not to mix with other children and he 'did not take to schooling.' He spoke Coptic, the native language of Egypt, and never learned to speak Greek. It is not even certain that he could read and write, although he certainly came to know the New Testament, the Psalms and a good deal of the other books of the Old Testament well enough to be able to quote from them freely. Before he was twenty his parents died, leaving a farm of over two hundred acres to him and his sister.

Saint Antony (II)
Vocation

One day, a few months after the death of his parents, he was on his way to church, thinking of how the apostles had left everything to follow our Lord, and how some of the first

Christians had sold everything to bring the money to the apostles. At Mass that day the Gospel was read about the rich young man whom our Lord told to 'sell all that you have; give the money to the poor; and come, follow me.'

As he was still responsible for his sister, Antony did not take this quite literally. He gave the land to the town authorities; he sold their house and belongings, and gave most of the money to the poor, but kept back a certain amount to take care of his sister.

Some while later he heard, in the Gospel at Mass, how our Lord had told his disciples to 'take no care for tomorrow'. This made him decide to keep back nothing of his own. He arranged for his sister to be brought up by a group of women whom we would now call nuns. No religious orders had yet been founded at that time; these ladies were probably living in private houses and arranging their lives in their own way to try to serve God. For himself Antony found a place to live outside the town and began a life of prayer and penance as a hermit.

The Ascetic Life

During the years of peace quite a number of good Christians felt that if they were not given an opportunity of martyrdom – an opportunity to die for Christ – they should at least 'take up their cross and follow him' by going into the desert as he had done, by living rough as he had done, by fasting, by 'chastising the body to bring it into obedience' as Saint Paul had done, by choosing to live as much as possible with and for Christ alone, as Mary, the sister of Martha and Lazarus, had chosen to do. Our Lord had told Martha that 'Mary had chosen the better part'.

Antony was not the only, nor the first, Christian hermit. There had been others from the time of John the Baptist although we have no proper records of them. Evidently Antony knew of some in his own district and he set himself to study their ways of life. He found work to do so as to earn bread for himself with something left over to give to the poor. He prayed constantly and in private. Our Lord had recommended us to 'pray in secret'. He listened carefully to the readings in church and memorised them so as to have no need of expensive books. He visited good and holy people round about so as to learn what he could from each.

Athanasius lists their virtues and practices: 'graciousness of one person, earnestness at prayer of another; good temper of one, kind heartedness of another; prayer and watching at night of one, studies of another; patient endurance of one, fasting and sleeping on the ground of another; gentleness of yet another. And in every one alike he noticed their devotion to Christ and their love for one another.' All these things he tried to imitate, but without upsetting anyone. The villagers where he lived 'called him "God's friend" and they became as fond of him as if he were one of the family.'

Saint Antony (III)
Attacks of the Devils

At this time more and more people were becoming Christians. The new Christians, remembering the persecutions which Decius and Valerian had started for the sake of the pagan religion, thought of the Roman pagan gods as cruel devils. Many Christians were superstitious and were afraid of these devils. The real devils, those about whom our Lord taught us, took advantage of this to try to frighten the Christians even more.

When we live on our own our imagination can play tricks on us. The devils also can use our imagination against us. God sometimes allows them to play tricks on us more directly, at times even using physical violence. So when Antony went to live alone in the desert Satan and his wicked angels attacked him in every way they could. They tried to tempt him with food and money and power, as they had tempted our Lord. They tempted him with women and the promise of luxury. In the end God even allowed them to try to terrorise him, to discourage him, and even to whip and beat him till one day he lost consciousness and lay half dead.

Saint Antony (IV)
In the Cemetery

Antony by this time had gone to live among the tombs in a cemetery. Some of these tombs were like vaults where many members of a family were buried in the same vault. He had shut himself up in one of these vaults with a door which locked from the outside. A friend had agreed to lock him in and to come back every few days with some bread to keep him alive.

The day after the devils had left him unconscious his friend came by with bread. When he unlocked the door he found Antony, still unconscious, lying on the ground. He picked him up and carried him to the village church. Some of Antony's relatives and friends in the village came and sat round his body, keeping watch, talking and praying. Towards midnight they had all fallen asleep except the one who had carried him into the church. Antony recovered consciousness though he was still very weak. He beckoned to his friend and got him to carry him back to the tomb. He was so weak he could neither walk nor stand. The friend left him there lying on the floor and praying. The door was locked on him again and he continued his battles with the fiends, but this time God sent him a vision of a light from heaven coming through the roof and a voice which promised him, 'I will always be your helper and I will make you renowned everywhere'. These things happened when he was about thirty-five years old.

Saint Antony (V)
In the Fort

The vision and the voice gave Antony new strength and encouragement. He decided to make a new start, further away from his family and the towns, but first he asked his friend to go with him. This friend, although he was still strong enough to carry Antony in his arms, was growing old. He did not think he was the right person to take part in Antony's venture, so Antony set off alone up the Nile. He crossed the river to the eastern bank and at a place called Pispir, about sixty miles south of the modern Cairo, he found a deserted fort where he decided to live. He obtained enough bread to last him for six months and then shut himself in, bricking up the door. People living in what Athanasius calls 'the house above' agreed to bring him a new supply of bread twice a year. He was able to receive this through a hole or window without opening the entrance; so he settled down to a life of solitary prayer, interrupted by more unsuccessful attacks from the devils. Altogether 'he spent nearly twenty years living the ascetic life by himself; never going out, and seldom seen by other people.'

The few people who did see him, or who spoke to him over the bricked up doorway, used to talk about him to others. More people began to visit the fort. Some asked him to pray for them. Some sick people were miraculously cured. Others began to imitate him, building cells for themselves in the hills and in the desert. These new hermits looked to Antony as their father and guide. At last some of his friends came and broke down the doorway and cleared it away.

Saint Antony (VI)
Recognising Spirits

Antony came out. To the surprise of all who saw him he was as healthy and strong as ever. Although he could not have had much exercise in his hermitage this had not made him flabby or weak. His years of fasting and his struggles with the devils had not made him shrivelled or wretched. In spirit too he was as kind and cheerful, as steady and sensible as he had ever been.

Athanasius gives in full a long sermon which Antony made to the monks and hermits around this time. His talk was chiefly about the ways in which devils can attack and tempt solitary Christians, trying to make them lose heart and give up. He explained particularly, from his own experience, how to recognise the more subtle temptations when the evil spirits quote scripture and pretend to be angels. When 'Christians, and especially monks, are working cheerfully and making progress' the devils try all sorts of different ways to attack them. But if their suggestions are worrying or disturbing – even if they seem to be holy, like urging us to pray longer or fast more – we should not listen to them. Once we are really growing in love of God the suggestions of the good spirit will be friendly and helpful. Any spirits which irritate and discourage us are likely to be evil, however much they quote scripture or pretend to be pious.

(Twelve hundred years later Saint Ignatius of Loyola taught us the same lesson. He also said that for people who have not made much progress – who are still easily tempted to sin – it is the temptations of the bad angels which seem pleasant, and the urgings of the good angels may seem disturbing and hard.)

Saint Antony (VII)
In Alexandria

In AD 305, when Diocletian and Maximian retired, Maximin Daia became Caesar under Galerius Augustus. Maximin was put in charge of Syria, Palestine and Egypt. He was a nephew of Galerius and a very harsh persecutor. Many of the terrible slaughterings and tortures seen or reported by Eusebius were undertaken under Maximin. During the persecution Antony left his cell and went to Alexandria. He hoped that he might be arrested; he visited the Christians in the mines and in the prisons. When they were condemned he went with them to the place of martyrdom and stayed by them, encouraging them and comforting them until they died. Other hermits or monks from the desert did the same until the senior judge ordered that all monks should be forbidden to appear in court and should be expelled from the city.

Antony then washed and bleached his clothes, and dressed himself like an ordinary Egyptian. Next day he went to the court again; he stood where the prefect could not avoid seeing him and prayed that he too might become a martyr. Even so the prefect did not arrest him, so he went on visiting, helping and comforting the confessors in prison as though he were one of them. Athanasius says he 'tired himself out in his toil for them'.

Saint Peter of Alexandria

Peter, the bishop of Alexandria, like Saint Cyprian of Carthage, had gone into hiding during the persecution; but a neighbouring bishop took the opportunity to interfere in Peter's diocese. He accused Peter of being too merciful to those who lapsed under persecution. Eusebius however says that Peter was a learned and wonderful Christian leader. He was martyred on 25th November 311.

Athanasius says that 'after Bishop Peter of blessed memory had suffered martyrdom, Antony left Alexandria and went back to his solitary cell.'

Saint Antony (VIII)
To the Inner Mountain

Back in his cell, Antony was again worried by visitors who believed that he could work miracles for them. Evidently many sick people were cured through his prayers. He tried to fix times for visitors and times when he could be free from disturbance. Once an officer called Martinianus came to him, insisting that he should come out to cure his daughter. Antony refused. 'I am a man,' he said, 'just as you are. If you believe in Christ whom I serve, go, and as you believe, pray to God. So it will happen.' The man did as Antony told him and his daughter was cured.

In time, visitors made it impossible for him to pray and meditate in solitude. He was also afraid that because God was working miracles through him, people would begin to say that it was he, Antony, who worked the miracles, and he would become proud. For these reasons he decided to go far up the river, partly to get away from distractions from people, and partly to avoid temptations to pride.

While he was waiting for one of the boats which sometimes passed, going upstream, he heard a voice asking where he was going, and why. 'The crowds do not allow me to be alone,' he answered. 'That is why I want to go to the Upper Thebaid, to escape all the annoyances here; and especially because people ask me to do things beyond my power.' 'If you really wish to be by yourself,' the voice replied, 'go up to the inner mountain.'

Antony had been brought up as an Egyptian town-dweller and did not know how to find his way through the desert away from the Nile. But he met a party of Arab nomads who were setting out to travel from the Nile to the Red Sea, going east. They allowed him to join them. For three days and nights he went along with them until they passed a high mountain with an oasis at the foot. In the oasis there were date palms and a spring of cold, clear fresh water. 'He fell in love with the place,' writes Athanasius, and he stayed there by himself, making it his new home. The Arabs left him a supply of bread. They admired him so much that they made a point of travelling the same route again from time to time, bringing more bread. He was also able, at the right season, to get dates from the palms. Eventually some of his friends who discovered where he had gone arranged a regular supply of food for him.

Saint Antony (IX)
Teacher and Leader

Antony soon felt that he was giving people too much trouble so he asked the monks to bring him some farm tools and some grain. With these he cultivated a small patch of land near the spring and grew enough food to feed himself. In time a few people found it possible to make the difficult journey, and they began to visit him again, though in smaller numbers than when he lived near the Nile. So he started to grow vegetables for his visitors.

He was already over sixty years old when he settled in this 'Inner Mountain' (it is called Mount Colzim), and as he grew older the monks who looked after him asked him to allow them to come every month, and bring him beans and some oil. Even so there was little food in the oasis. Visitors now were fewer. Antony had more time for prayer to God – and for more fights with the devils. But the monks and hermits in the 'Outer Mountain' near the Nile needed his guidance and advice. They sent two or three monks to ask him to come and visit them. He agreed. While they were travelling west, with a camel carrying the provisions for their journey, their water ran out. They almost died, and they let the camel go. Antony went aside to pray, and presently they found a spring. Eventually they also caught the camel again and were able to reach the communities by the Nile in safety.

Besides visiting the monks, Antony also went to see his sister who was now 'grown old in her virginity, herself the guiding spirit of other virgins'. He stayed some days with the groups near the river. When he went back to the Inner Mountain he realised that God wished him to be a leader for others and he became less unapproachable than he had been before. More people made the difficult journey to his oasis. Saint Athanasius may have been among them since he writes, word for word, some of the advice which Antony gave his visitors. Others went to him to be cured of diseases or helped in their troubles.

Athanasius describes several of the miracles which occurred, giving the names and details of those who were helped. In each case Antony insisted that he himself had no power of healing. He preferred it when the sick people did not come to him but only sent someone to ask for his prayers. In one case a sick girl was brought to the foot of the mountain with her parents and waited there while friends spoke to Antony. He would not allow the others to come up. 'Go,' he said, 'You will find her cured if she has not died. This is no work of mine. Her cure is the work of the Saviour. He shows his mercy everywhere to those who call on him.'

As well as working miracles in answer to Antony's prayers, God sent him visions. But despite these visions and the miracles, Antony always showed great respect for priests and deacons. When it came to prayers he always asked a priest or a deacon to lead. He was always ready to learn from others. Only heretics he preferred to avoid unless he saw an opportunity to urge them back into the Catholic Church.

Saint Antony (X)
In Alexandria again

At one time the Arians in Alexandria tried to make out that Antony held the same ideas about our Lord's nature as they had.

The bishops and other Catholics appealed to him to come to Alexandria to refute this lie. He came to the city and preached there publicly. He taught the people that 'the Son of God is the eternal Word and Wisdom of the substance of the Father.'

Many of the pagans, and even some of the pagan priests in Alexandria came to listen to him. Some asked to be allowed to touch him because they could feel his goodness. In the few days that he stayed in the city there were as many new converts to Christianity as were normally baptised in a whole year.

'When he was leaving,' writes Athanasius, 'and we were seeing him off, a woman behind us cried out, "Wait, man of God. Please wait or I shall hurt myself running. My daughter is tormented by a devil." We begged him to stop; he did so gladly. When the woman came up to us her child was hurled to the ground. Antony prayed and called on the name of Christ. The child stood up cured. The mother praised God, and we all gave thanks. He too was glad as he left to go back to the mountain. For him that was his home.'

Saint Antony (XI)
Last Years

Towards the end of his life Antony visited the Outer Mountain more often. During these visits Greek and Egyptian philosophers came, amongst other people, to talk to him. Although he had to use an interpreter to translate between Coptic and Greek he was able to meet their philosophic arguments so cleverly, yet so pleasantly, that they were both embarrassed and pleased at the same time. He showed how faith in our Lord is better than any philosophy. They were impressed by his arguments and could not help feeling that the miracles performed through him seemed to confirm the truth of his beliefs. 'They admired him,' writes Athanasius. 'As they left they embraced him. They acknowledged that they had been helped by him.'

The Emperor Constantine, and his sons Constantius and Constans, wrote to Antony. He did not like receiving letters from such exalted people; but his friends told him he ought to reply, so he wrote back, reminding them that Christ alone is the true and eternal King. He urged them to be humane and just, and to help the poor.

Constantine, in AD 335, had been persuaded to exile Athanasius from Alexandria, but the bishop was allowed to return in 337. It was probably in that year that Antony visited Alexandria to speak against the Arians. Also in 337 Constantine died. He had never really appreciated the importance of the dispute over the Arian heresy. Constantius, the next emperor, favoured the Arians much more than his father had done. Athanasius was banished again in 339 and went to Rome. He was unable to return to Alexandria until 346. About the year 354 Antony, out in the desert, saw a terrible vision of a new persecution of the Catholics, not this time by the pagans, but by the Arian heretics.

Athanasius, writing three years later, described what Antony had told to those who were with him at the time of the vision. 'Wrath is going to strike the Church,' he said. 'I saw the table of the Lord's house with mules around it, standing in a ring, kicking up their hooves at what was there – like the kicking when a herd runs wild.' After the vision he heard a voice which said, 'My altar will be desecrated'.

'And two years later', continues Athanasius, 'came the present persecution by the Arians and the plundering of the churches. They took the vessels by force and had them carried away by pagans. They forced the pagans from their shops and made them come to their meetings. In front of the pagans they did as they pleased with the sacred table. Then we all realised that the kicking of the mules, foreseen by Antony, was what the Arians were doing now like so many senseless animals.'

Pope Liberius and all the important Catholic bishops of the west were thrown out of their sees. The emperor sent soldiers to arrest Athanasius, but he escaped. It was while he was in hiding that Athanasius wrote the life of Antony.

Saint Antony (XII)
The Physician of Egypt

His monks were not the only people who were sometimes able to persuade Antony into journeying as far as the Outer

Mountain. At one time the judges needed his advice. They sent some of the defendants in cases before their courts to his oasis and told them to beg his help in making sure they obtained justice. Those who were sick, or their friends, kept coming to beg him to heal them. He would never do more than advise them and pray, calling on the name of Christ, so as to show that it was not he – Antony – who made them well. It was our Lord showing his loving kindness.

A Roman commander, Balacius, who supported the Arians, was so brutal to the monks and nuns that Antony wrote to him to warn him that God's judgement would fall on him. Balacius threw the letter on the ground and spat on it. Five days later his horse, who had always been a most gentle animal, attacked the commander, bit him, threw him down, and savaged his thigh so badly that he died three days afterwards.

Good people who came to Antony with their troubles all found help. He was like a doctor, wrote Athanasius, given by God to the land of Egypt. The sad came away from him cheerful; the sick came away healed; those who were quarrelling came away friends. Many who came to listen to him decided to give their lives to God and became monks or nuns.

Saint Antony (XIII)
Happy Death

On one of his visits to the Outer Mountain Antony said that he felt like a fish out of water, longing to get back to the sea. During his last visit he told the monks, 'It is now time for me to die. I am nearly a hundred and five years old.' They urged him to stay and spend his last days with them, but he refused. One reason was because the Christians in Egypt kept up the old Egyptian custom of mummifying the bodies of those whom they specially loved and respected. They would even keep the mummies in their own homes. Antony disapproved.

When he was back in his oasis, with the two monks who took care of him in his last years, he told them they must bury him in the earth secretly and not let anyone know where he was laid. He told them to give to Bishop Athanasius his cloak and one of his sheepskins which the bishop had given him some years before. The other sheepskin he told them to give to Bishop Serapion, the bishop of Thmuis in the Nile delta. Serapion when young had been a follower of Saint Antony in the desert, and was a great friend and supporter of Athanasius. His hair shirt they were to keep themselves. Then he blessed them and kissed them. He drew his feet up onto the couch. With a happy look on his face, as though he was full of joy, meeting old friends, he lay down and died.

This was in the year 356. In 357 Athanasius received a letter from 'friends in a foreign country' – he does not say where – asking him to write a life of Antony. Athanasius had with him one of the monks who had been close to Antony for a long time. From his personal knowledge – 'I have seen him often,' he wrote – and from what he learned from this companion, Athanasius was able to write the 'Life of Saint Antony' which we read today.

The Age of the Fathers of the Church

Athanasius at this time was sixty or sixty-one years old. He died sixteen years later; but his exciting life belongs to a new age of the Church. There were still martyrdoms from time to time. Some of the Christian emperors were more troublesome than the milder pagan emperors had been. But our interest in the fourth and fifth centuries is not so much in courage of the Christians under persecution. It is more in the development of the study and the practice of Christ's teaching by the great 'Fathers of the Church', the great Christian writers: Athanasius, Basil, Gregory of Nazianzus and John Chrysostom writing in Greek; Jerome, Ambrose, Augustine and – later – Gregory the Great writing in Latin.

Antony belongs to both ages – or to neither. He was born before the death of Cyprian. He lived through the great persecutions of Diocletian, Galerius and Maximin. He was sixty-two when Constantine abolished the laws against Christianity, and he lived through the earlier troubles with the Arian heretics. But his real interest for us is in his being the first of the long line of monks and nuns about whom we know enough to feel we can really know and love him as a person.

Apostles and Martyrs

The *Life of Saint Antony* by Saint Athanasius is the first book after the New Testament which has drawn generations of good men and women to choose the religious life, leaving the world so as to work more single-mindedly in the service of God.

> '*O God, you enlighten our minds with the gift of your Holy Spirit; grant that by the light of the same Spirit we may always be wise so as to love your goodness, shown in your saints and martyrs, and to enjoy the consolations of your Spirit in our hearts.*'